FIRE & ASH

THE ALCHEMY OF CANCER

CHRISTINE SHERWOOD

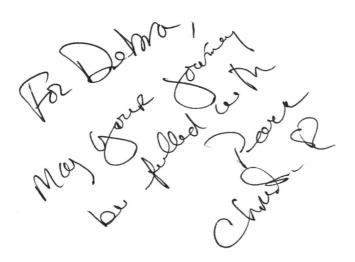

For Debra!
May your journey
be filled with
Peace
Christine

"Christine Sherwood vividly brings us into her world, balancing the darkness with the light, inspired by deep faith, love, and trust in the divine plan for her life. She shares the compelling story in moving prose and poetry of how she found her way through a most demanding physical, emotional and spiritual journey catalyzed by cancer. She finds her refuge and the divine in her heart and soul."

— LUCILLE MARCHAND, BSN, M.D., Director of the Palliative Care Program, University of Washington Medical Center

"With spare and elegant prose, Christine Sherwood gathers us up and carries us into the fire of her encounter with death, and then lifts us out of the ashes and delivers us into the quiet radiance of her transformed life. Masterfully done."

— MIRABAI STARR, author of *God of Love: A Guide to the Heart of Judaism, Christianity and Islam*

"...Sherwood's epic journey is not a "medical procedural" or a "cancer story." It is a universally inspiring Hero's Journey as she confronts the post-illness questions so many people grapple with: Who am I now? How shall I live? How can I help others face and answer these questions? Sherwood takes us on her journey to hell and back to health in lucid, highly refined prose."

— STEVE FOX, author of *Odyssey: Love and Terror in Greece, 1969*

"With raw honesty and vulnerability, Christine Sherwood explores the truth of all spiritual teachings: that contained within every human experience—even cancer—lies the potential for deep connection with the Divine."

— KAREN BALDWIN, cancer bloomer and author of *Ruby's World—My Journey with the Zulu*

"Christine Sherwood is a very brave and fine woman. May her heart touch thousands of others. All stories form the river that carry us on." — DANIEL LADINSKY, bestselling Penguin author

FIRE & ASH
THE ALCHEMY OF CANCER

©2014 Christine Sherwood
All rights reserved.

ISBN Number: 978-0692328590
Library of Congress Control Number: 2014956386

Printed in the United States of America

Cover art: Tal Walton
Painting photograph: Lucia Young
Author photograph: Chaitanyo

To contact the author, visit
www.christine-sherwood.com

For information, contact Nighthawk Press:
www.nighthawkpress.com

NIGHTHAWK PRESS
TAOS, NEW MEXICO

Ivy loves the branchless willow and the old trunk of the oak in spring. Cancer is like that strange plant—it attaches itself and clings to the people who lived good and generous lives.
VINCENT VAN GOGH

Dedicated to the memory of
Judy, Julie and Lisa,
and
to all those who have
burned
in the fire of cancer.

About the Cover Art
Passage, by Tal Walton

"Throughout our lives, passages manifest themselves
in diverse ways. Oftentimes, we arrive someplace new, not
knowing what lies just beyond the opening. Fear prevents some
from crossing into the unknown, while others step through
with anxious purpose. We each experience passages that are
unique to our existence—some sought after, others stumbled
upon, and some forced upon us—each holding in common
a change, a purpose, and an increase in wisdom."

Tal Walton's paintings can be found in private
and corporate collections throughout the world, as well
as museums in the United States. He currently lives
with his family in the foothills of northern Colorado.

ACKNOWLEDGMENTS

First and foremost, I give thanks to my beloved spiritual teachers, whose grace inspired and guided this book. I humbly bow to your presence in my life.

To my fellow human travelers, I am gratefully indebted.

My publisher, Rebecca Lenzini, and editors Barbara Scott and David Scott were pillars of support throughout the writing of this book. Their expertise, friendship, and laughter gave me the courage to continue writing.

Bountiful thanks to my parents, Jean and Gil, who believed in me from the start; and to my daughter, Tracy, who is one of my best teachers; to Nia White, for her profound friendship and listening to hours of my process, and to John Richardson, who compelled me to write this book.

A passage in the *I Ching* reads, "Our lives are shaped by those who love us and by those who refuse to love us." This is certainly true in my life. Fortunately, I am blessed with many who love me and teach me through their compassion and kindness. To the family members, friends, healers, nurses, doctors, and strangers who are not mentioned in the book – but who played major and minor roles in this story of cancer and healing – I am truly thankful. I wish I could have mentioned each and every one of you, but you are in this book because you are in my heart.

Special appreciation to René Janiece, who produced the Kickstarter project that financially supported me through the year of writing this book. And to the generous contributions of Martha and Chris Flanders, Jean and Gil Schwantes, Mike and Kathy Schwantes, Kathi Ragan, Korri Ragan, Carol Slaven, Gary Gibson, Justin Idione, and Rebecca Lenzini, along with the many other people who made the project successful. Many thanks.

To all of you, my heartfelt gratitude, for your unwavering belief in me. I know that I accomplish nothing on my own but rather through the connection we all share.

Namaste

Go ahead, light your candles and burn your incense
and ring your bells and call out to God, but watch out,
because God will come and He will put you on
His anvil and fire up His forge and beat you and beat you
until He turns you into pure gold.

SANT KESHAVADAS

PROLOGUE

It is late at night, around midnight, and the doctor is standing at the side of my hospital bed. He's checking in on me, because for the second time in two weeks, I've almost died of an abdominal infection. We're waiting for the ambulance to take me to Albuquerque, where the original surgeon will diagnose the problem.

I am agitated but lucid: "I'm going to live through this," I tell the doctor. "And when I do, I'm going to finish school and help other cancer patients to understand that there is a language of fear associated with cancer. I'm going to support integrating holistic and Western medicine, for the benefit of all involved in this disease. Because of the suspicion and lack of communication between these two worlds, I feel I have had a foot in two boats. It is exhausting, and it has nearly cost me my life."

The doctor listens, and when I'm finished reporting my future plans, he says, "You sure aren't talking like a person who's dying."

INTRODUCTION

I am the Soul of a human being. I exist within the Soul of the Universe. I have no shape or form. I am free, but I have a purpose: to dwell within the body of a human being. I am everywhere, at all times and in all dimensions. Though I am always united with the Soul of the Universe, I serve a human being for the purpose of our allied freedom. We are bound together in this journey to be lifted into Universal Love, where we experience connection to the divinity of our birthright. I have many tools at my disposal to fulfill my purpose, which is to open a human heart. I use each one with great mastery revealed through me by Christ, the Divine Mother, Krishna, Buddha, and all the Gods and Goddesses of Eternity.

One of my many tools is cancer.

Success or failure is not my true concern; I ask each human being to participate with me in his or her unique way, with a most authentic voice. That is how samsara—the recurring bondage of the human experience—is released: through pure authenticity. It is only misunderstanding in the human mind that attaches itself to outcomes. God is eternally merciful and forgiving.

Cultivating detachment and compassion is no small challenge, for human beings are wrought with carefully placed fears. As these wounds are absolved, Creation, in its receptive rapture, delights in the reconciliation of the human heart to its one true home. Suffering is the vehicle that conveys humans to this precious homecoming. Some deny suffering, at too high a cost. They cannot hear the calling of their Soul to risk the full surrendering of the body. Many believe that death is a failure, when in truth it is what humans live for; it is that which guides them to be kind and honest. It creates an urgency to come into communion with God.

In accepting the body's inevitable demise, they develop true compassion; this, in turn, diminishes the separation they feel—between genders, races, and countries—to experience oneness. All people are one; each has a Soul connection and each longs for the same love and belonging necessary to find happiness within the confines of this life. Everything that happens in a person's life belongs to them. Life cannot be lived wrongly, for every path, every living connection made, leads us home.

I am indebted to the being in whose service I work. This being of whom I speak does not yet understand the degree to which we reverberate, in tandem, off the walls of God to find each other. This being feels separate and alone at this moment, but this is far from the truth. I have been given the duty of the witness, the guide and the benefactor to this being. The body of this being is in the female aspect, and I will call her by her Soul name, Nilama. NEE-la-ma.

Like every other being, her body is the discrete form of her Soul, a condensation of my attributes. The Universe revels in the creation of life. It celebrates the coming home that Nilama does not yet have the imagination for. She longs to be free of the human suffering she has seen and felt, to be united with the wisdom of the ages, to belong once again to the compassion her heart remembers. Nilama is not ready for the ultimate merging; it is not her time to be fully taken by death, but she continues to pray for the under-standing of how to be at home in the body. I am calling Nilama to know me—to express my purpose through her—and she is respond-

ing to the call. It is necessary for me to choose a tool with which to instruct. It must be a powerful tool, for she is earnest in her quest for love, and I believe she is ready.

I choose cancer as her catalyst for change. It is my solemn oath to remain by her side, to open a heart that has been wounded by its very birth, to offer her the gift of awakening. I am duty bound to ensure that Nilama will begin to envision the Truth, to experience the light in the darkness she is about to enter, to see that cancer is the messenger, not the message.

I know the torture of her experience. She will wrestle with her demons. Doubt the existence of God. Deem herself not worthy of love. Then implode into a tight feeling of abandonment and fierce, unrelenting pain. She will be angry and grieve over perceived losses and rage against the dying of the light. But I know that relenting will serve her better. I do not fear for her. I already know how this will play out.

Throughout her journey, I will be whispering to her; gentle words will brush her cheek late in the night. When she cries out in an ambulance, I will dance before her. When she is near death in her sick bed, I will send the angels to carry her through. In surgery, I will inspire the breath of life back into her, and when she can take no more and resolves to end her life, I will send her daughter's laughter to break the fever of defeat. She will hear me, feel me, know me. As veil upon veil is removed to expose her tender heart, I will remain always with her, applying the soothing balm of Love. I will employ many willing Souls to support her on her journey. So, dear ones, have faith: all is well, and will be well.

I have noted Nilama's love of words—perhaps poetry will be the dynamic structure for my purpose...

ONE

Something wants to come through me. Phrases are forming in my mind and demanding attention. I have written a few poems. This process is new to me and I am fascinated by what emerges on the page. I sense that these poems will heal me, give me a voice through which to process my experience. I have been so consumed by the dark night of the Soul in these past months of cancer that it's surprising to feel any sort of creative inspiration.

I have a three-month respite until the ileostomy reversal. In order to heal the interior surgery from last February, a procedure called an ileostomy took place, in which a loop of the ileum was pulled through the abdominal wall. This "stoma" releases feces into a bag on the outside of the body, keeping the colon empty. I have been given these months to rebuild my strength from chemo and radiation treatments and from surgery. In May, I will finally succumb to what I believe is the last invasion of my body. Then I can begin to put all of this behind me. I am anxious to get back to my life.

Winter is beginning to loosen its grip and release itself into spring. What a winter it has been, the brittle cold compounding the scourge of chemotherapy, radiation, and major surgery — all of it requiring more from me than

I thought my body and spirit could endure. Judy has come to be with me, her third visit. She has built a fire in the wood stove. Having recovered enough from February's surgery, I'm finally able to be up from bed, and as we sit in the living room, I read her a piece from my first poem:

⁂

Life seemed to co-operate with my every move
What grace, gratitude and joy!
I wanted to experience it all
And God said: All right my child
Here also is pain
Here also is great suffering
And just to make sure you know it intimately
I will give it a name
Cancer
It will tear you where you don't have seams
Eat the flesh from your bones
And leave them bleached white by the desert sun
How fast can you move now?
What is the pace of the human soul when all else is
        stripped away?
I was always in such a hurry
But now perhaps I'll find a new stride
So that death's experience of me is like the walking rain
On the distant plains
Inevitable
But
Gentle and slow to come near

⁂

We pause in silence as the power of the words encircles us. Judy gently looks up at me, a tone of empathy filling her voice, as she simply says, "Keep writing." I realize now that I should listen carefully to this new language beginning to speak through me, for I am not the same. My life as I have known it has been impossibly changed.

TWO

I am walking down the hallway in the doctor's office, desensitized, caught up in a whirlwind of thoughts. The doctor I saw six months ago, before the diagnosis, is walking toward me, and I notice her attention directed at me. When she is close enough, she says, in a confessional voice, "I'm very sorry. I didn't do right by you when you came to see me. I could have done more for you, listened better, and I didn't."

During that visit I had been concerned about how tired I was feeling, about my hair falling out, my irregular digestive patterns, the pain in my sacral region. No, I had not lost weight, and I was aware that to the naked eye, I would have appeared to be in excellent health...

My response to her now was flat, but sincere in its lack of blame. "It's OK. You weren't the only one." I would report these same symptoms to acupuncturists, chiropractors, and even a blood specialist, who said, "Don't worry. Whatever it is, it's not serious or it would have shown up in your blood." The diagnosis I was given by most was that, at age forty-eight, I was entering menopause.

Cancer is cunning.

Two weeks earlier, I met the stranger who would change my life. I saw it on the screen above my head during the endoscopy. It looked like a huge, ulcerous canker, tucked into all that perfect pink interior tissue. It looked menacing and took up real space inside of me. Nothing about the moment could be denied: I had seen it with my own eyes, and I knew my life was going to change in ways I could not imagine.

With a diagnosis of third-stage rectal cancer a week later, I suddenly had much more to tend to than misdiagnoses from the estranged participants of my now very distant past. Nothing but my focus on the present crisis deemed itself worthy of energy. I felt caught up in a strange flow, far beyond my control.

⟉⟎⟍⟎⟐⟎⟍⟎⟊

I thought it could never happen to me
Then one day the tag on the back of my shirt caught the
     edge of the tornado
I was in flight before my wings could open
But as it turned out they weren't needed
I was kept moving by a violent benevolent force
I knew the peace in the eye of the tornado was just a
     breath away
But there was no movement of the lungs that could
     physically move me into that calm
There was no silver blade that could slice the congested air
     and make it clear again
There was only dodging the obstacles as they crashed
     about me
Honing a deeper intuition of when to duck to avoid being
     knocked into another tailspin

And knowing that even this could not be avoided
I must become the tailspin
Inhale what is given
Catch the prayer beads thrown into the wind by hands
    of love

·⤳⚉⤳·

It felt like divine intervention when, on the evening of the diagnosis, before going home alone, I sat with my friend Jean and her husband, a physician at a hospital in Albuquerque. Jean had been with me for support in the doctor's office and rarely left my side from that day onward. Her husband told me he knew a surgeon and called him that very evening. By chance, the surgeon had recently returned from the Mayo Clinic, where he'd studied the latest surgical procedure for rectal cancer, a procedure it appeared I was going to need. While the two physicians were in conversation, it was revealed that the surgeon worked with an oncologist who was currently looking for candidates to join a study for the very type of cancer I had. It was proclaimed that I would join others in his experiment.

Jean's husband continued to make calls that evening, and by Monday I was in the system and being prepped for five weeks of daily chemo and radiation, followed by a surgery to remove part of my rectum, which would leave me with an ileostomy. Finally, I would undergo a reversal of that ileostomy and be returned to normal.

The urgency of the late-stage diagnosis dictated the pace and influenced many of my decisions. I was told that I would be cured if I followed the protocol presented to me.

The word "cured" got my full attention. My doctor in Taos, Larry Schreiber, who gave me the original diagnosis, had said with a regretful voice: "Sometimes bad things happen to good people." He has known me through my healing work in town, and he gave me this cautious advice: "You can do all the holistic treatments you like, but if you want to live, do everything they're telling you to do."

Although I had no sense of what lay ahead, I began the tumultuous journey.

The most difficult person to share the news with was my daughter, Tracy. The previous July, we had driven together to Pasadena, where she had begun pastry-chef school at Le Cordon Bleu. When she heard the news, she said through her tears, "I'm coming home!" I told her that would not be necessary, that I would be all right; from the beginning, I had the intuitive sense that I would live. (Does everyone have this feeling?) She should continue with her dream. Going to Le Cordon Bleu brought a light into Tracy's eyes, which I believed could only be illuminated by a true calling. As we talked, she relented but made me promise that if I was going to die I would call her. In complete shock and naïveté, I agreed to this plan. How could I know the sinister scheme not yet revealed? Looking back at the times I almost died, I never would have been able to keep my promise.

The only other person with whom I remember having much of a conversation about the cancer was my mother on the day I received the diagnosis. I was in the front seat of my friend's car, on her cell phone, in the parking lot of the hospital. My mother, also in shock but looking for a silver lining (and I'm sure protecting me in the same way I was protecting my daughter), said, "Oh, don't worry. The tumor is so close to the outside of your body, they'll just go right up there and snip it out!"

Unfortunately, this wasn't even close to what they had in mind.

This was on October 18, 2006. The events of the following years would be unrecognizable compared to the trajectory I had thought my life would follow. I would lose most of what I had spent my life's work creating, except for those truths that nothing can destroy. Some relationships would be demolished as new ones formed. Love would manifest from the fire of transformation, fiercely determined to reshape me, and I would participate. God help me, I would participate with all my heart and soul.

∞

As the Soul, I do not know all the twists and turns of the story until they unfold, because a human being has free will. We weave the intricate outcome of an experience together, along with other Souls, every being playing its part, perfectly in character. The lessons of the participants are intertwined for the good of all.

THREE

I'm lying back in a La-Z-Boy recliner, facing the window. I'm looking out at the trees, set in place for my benefit: They give way to the onset of winter in the same way I've surrendered years of avoiding drugs to the onslaught of invasive chemotherapy. I'm receiving the dangerous potion through a port near my clavicle, imagining the golden light of God filtering into my veins, His infinite wisdom knowing what to kill and what to leave unharmed. This is more than a prayer: I am faced with a crucible that will take all my years of spiritual practice to accomplish.

In the yoga I study, one of the main teachings is that everything and everyone is God. God dwells in the human heart, the trees, the wind, and the unlit match. Which means that the chemo and radiation I've agreed to receive *is* God, and so is the cancer. To fully embrace the sacred words of masters throughout the lineage of time, the cancer cannot be excluded. I welcome the teaching wholeheartedly; the urgency of the situation allows no space for doubt. I've been toying with this truth for years, and the dress rehearsal is over. Either I will employ this truth with confidence or I will suffer mentally and resist the very thing offered to save my life.

There's no evident reason for cancer to have usurped my body with such a vengeance. My diet and lifestyle for the past thirty years have supported vibrant health. I acknowledged long ago that my body is a temple, housing the mysterious human potential to unite in unconditional love with the source that created me. Even taking an aspirin used to give me pause. And now I was allowing some of the most fearsome drugs on Earth into my veins.

There are judgments from some of the people I know, fed by these fears, about the treatments I'm choosing. They don't believe in this course of action. I should do macrobiotics, they say. Go to Mexico. Anything but have my body devoured by chemo and radiation, then cut open with parts removed. I wish they could feel the crushing pain in my rectum, the fear coursing through my nervous system, and the instinct to live driving me into unfamiliar territory — all housed in the grace that is guiding me into this potent interior struggle between darkness and light.

I wish they could let go of disembodied emotions (and their own fears) and join me in closing the gap between *what is God* and *what is not*. Some of these people will find the courage to travel the undetermined, mystical road of cancer with me. They will honor my decision to stay in Taos, will drive me to treatments sixty miles away, will feed me. They will touch, hold and heal my ravaged body, support me while I build altars for the daily chemo pills, enticing the Goddess to bless these dark allies that I intend to ingest.

Nilama and I are expanding as her faith in herself widens. She is hearing with her heart. Fear is running rampant and clouding her mind, but a resolute trust reigns within. Even though she believes that all her trust in God is in question, faith will serve her now and always, for the work of the human heart is never lost. Nilama is opening herself to my interventions and, through cancer, allowing Grace to bring understanding.

FOUR

I arrive at the cancer center only to find that the radiation machine is not functioning and I won't get my treatment today. It's somewhere around day fifteen, and friends have been driving me from Taos to Santa Fe every day for five weeks of twenty-five treatments, ninety minutes each way. This doesn't sit well with me. I don't want to do this one day longer than planned.

I've grown close to the people at the center, particularly the two women who work in the radiation department. They give me the news in the treatment room. While listening, an idea pops into my head, and I speak it aloud: "Let me do Reiki on this machine." Surprisingly, they agree, and I tell them they must leave the room for me to initiate the process. I've seen Reiki perform miracles before—why not now? I feel a strange mix of desperation and faith. I plant my feet facing the monstrous machine in the middle of the room. It is cold in here. My hands glide through the air, half-confident that this will work.

It takes less than a minute to accomplish the act, then the technicians return to the room and try the machine. It works!

I do not feel personally responsible for this marvel. I feel humbled by powers I don't understand but strive to believe in. I'm astonished and a little numb; at another time this may have brought awe but right in this moment, all I can think about is what I have to do next. The voice inside me is not surprised, and I hear, *"Well, of course it worked. I am real."*

I'm relieved to get my treatment. Adhering to the schedule gives me a false sense of control, and I say to the techs, "Now everyone else can get their treatments today, too." There seems no greater task at hand than to complete this protocol; in my impatience, I may have missed the gift I was just given.

A week or so later, second-degree radiation burns cover my genitals, anus and thighs — inside and out. I'm in the kind of pain I could never have imagined. I am sick, weak, and losing faith in the meditations I've been practicing while receiving radiation.

On my next visit, once again the machine is not working, and we've already traveled the distance to reach the center. The techs suggest I try Reiki again. I'm obliged to do so, but now I wish this was all over and I'd never have to look at this apparatus again. Maybe if it doesn't work I could quit and go home and all this would end. I'm on liquid morphine, along with a cocktail of other drugs, for the burn pain. But nothing seems to take the pain away; the drugs only make me not care that I'm in ferocious pain.

I perform the Reiki symbols; the ancient swirls and lines caress open space, and once again the machine works. "Wow, we should be paying you to sit in the corner with your good energy and keep the machine going," the techs exclaim. "You're more reliable than the guys who come to

fix it!" With a twisted sense of humor I say, "The least
you could do is give me free treatments in payment for
my service." I can actually laugh, but there's a disconnect
within me—some unknowable discord. I never could have
imagined that the modalities I have learned over the past
decades would be put to task in this way. Is there a difference between a machine and a human being? After all,
we're made up of the same thing...energy. But my firm
beliefs about what's right and compassionate are chafing
against my realigned understanding.

The treatments are taking me down. To my original
twenty-five radiation treatments, the doctors want to add
three more that will directly target the tumor. I'm supposed
to be done on a Thursday, and this extension would take
me through to the next Tuesday, adding insult to injury.
Each treatment worsens the burns, and on Friday, while
I'm getting the first of my additional treatments, I confess
to the techs that I will not return on Monday, or any other
day, to do any more. I have had all I can take. They understand my decision, and while I'm lying outside the machine,
where usually they mark the guides with black magic mark-
ers to line up the radiation, they are drawing poinsettias and
Christmas ornaments on my belly—even HO HO HO!—
in red and green and blue. As I walk out of that steel room,
they play the graduation march. I am beyond happy to
walk out of there, but this doesn't feel like a celebration,
only a completion ill suited for joy.

Pain is robbing me of perspective. I know that recent
events surpass average human powers, but I can't feel the
mystery in them. I feel flat and scared. Anxiety has taken

hold of faith and sent it on its way. I don't stop my meditations, though, and while confined to bed for endless hours, I continue to wear headphones playing sacred chants that echo in my mind. I don't feel God's presence, but I won't stop calling out. Maybe this is true faith. The meaning of words I understood so assuredly before cancer—words like love and faith and compassion—now eludes me. Today those definitions are being tempered on harder ground, and that ground is me. I am learning that to observe suffering in another and to be on the receiving end of suffering are very different propositions. It's hard to process what I'm being asked to go through. But something urges me on and I must follow, though I don't know where I'm being led. And in a way I don't care anymore. Maybe I'm learning to surrender.

Every human being is born whole and complete. But in order to fully understand this, each first must experience life in all its terrible beauty and complexity. Nilama is not as close to real surrender as she thinks; a long, difficult road lies ahead, and her journey has just begun. I will thread her through the eye of the needle. It will be a perilous journey, but through this narrow opening is her true home.

FIVE

I need to go to the emergency room; the burns are unbearable. But I cannot drive myself to the hospital, which compounds my sense of panic. I've been on the phone, trying to reach nurses overloaded with patients who have taken precedence over me — I have been usurped by those in greater need. Having been at the top of the list for months, I never imagined losing my seniority, and in my piercing pain and anxiety, I feel abandoned.

I make frantic calls to friends, and at first I can't reach anyone for a ride. Finally, I get in touch with Helen. "Hold on, I'm on my way," she says calmly. Helen is one of those friends who, just by being in the room, can alter the fear factor in me. I also call Selah for help, with no answer, but now he has returned my call and he, too, will arrive soon. Selah has been coming to my house two or three times a week to give me acupuncture treatments; maybe he can bring this pain to a reasonable level. I breathe a little easier. Wait, Walter is here also... Did I call him, too?

With my friends near me, I am calmer now, grateful to have help. I lie down on my belly, in my bed. The pain is in my rectal area, and there's no room for modesty. Selah is putting needles into extremely sensitive places. Helen is holding my head and Walter my feet. I'm losing track of the pain's epicenter because my skin has become a blanket of raw nerve endings.

I melt a little into the hands of my friends, into the trust I have for them and the love they offer me. They help me remember to breathe. I don't know if it's taken five minutes or an hour for the pain to subside, but it does. Praise Goddess, I am spared going to the hospital.

By the way, I have a crush on Selah. I know he has a girlfriend, but how can I help it? He has visited my sickbed for months, graciously telling me stories to distract me from the pain. One day, when death seems like a kind alternative to the suffering, he tells me the story of Pandora's box, then looks at me with great compassion and says, "Not even hope, Christine. Not even hope can you hold onto." I had never known that it was *hope* that Pandora trapped in the box, but I'm unable to take in this Buddhist teaching. I want to hope, I want to believe, to control what I can in my healing or my dying, even if it's through denial. If I lose these allies, how can I endure another minute? I lie silent on the table as he finishes his work, not in as much pain but no less terrified about this life-and-death dilemma in which I find myself.

Some months later, after February's major surgery, I'm sitting in my living room with Helen; she has spent the night once again. We face each other from couch to chair. In my exhaustion I feel like a corpse that continues on, fueled by pain. I look at Helen and say, "I don't believe in God anymore. How could a benevolent God allow such things to happen? None of this is OK with me. None of this is OK at all. There is no God."

⁓⊰⊱⁓

I swirl into deep dark dungeons
I am shackled by my blindness
The danger is a hot, musty breath on the back of my neck
I want to run, but there is no ground
Scream, but there is no voice

⁓⊰⊱⁓

The spiritual crisis has begun. The alchemy of transmutation takes time and pressure. As Nilama calls out to God with her doubtful prayers, her cries of grief and anger, the precise fuel for the flame of the Master's forge, her raw metal is laid on the anvil of life to be beaten and beaten into a transparent sheet of gold.

I rest beside Nilama late one night, anguished questions rattling through her mind, pleading for understanding. I am moved to provide some solace, for my compassionate heart beats within hers, and we share this journey. I say with complete conviction and truth, "This is what you came for."

Nilama hears these words and takes them into herself, letting them settle into her spirit and body, testing the truth against the hard judge of her nervous system. The neurotransmitters respond with their verdict. "Yes," Nilama says to herself, "for this I was born." And a mist of peace settles over her heart.

.

SIX

My daughter, Tracy, and I are under the covers, with winter hats on our heads, candles glowing, in an unheated motel room. Once again there is no electricity, due to the massive winter storm raging from Albuquerque to Texas. It is New Year's Eve and we're grateful to have the shelter. Apparently we snagged the last room in town. This scenario creates a moment for us to bond in a way that we have not yet done through the cancer.

We are on the return trip from a Christmas visit to my parents' home in Wisconsin. My father had pleaded with me to come home one evening, a night when going to the bathroom was like passing razor blades, and I had been on the bathroom floor throbbing in pain from the burns over which I could gain no authority. I had called my parents in a state of desperation and agreed to come home. When next I spoke with Tracy, she offered to fly to New Mexico, meet me at the airport, and do this together.

I need help. I need my family around me. As thoughts of home generate the energy I need to pull off this trip, once again I'm torn between being in Wisconsin or in my own home, in my own bed, back in Taos. Should I stay in Wisconsin to finish the protocol? This is an improbable scenario, and I do my best to weigh the facts. In Wisconsin, I would have my parents to rely on (but they're almost eighty years old), and I do have a few siblings still in the area. Could they do the job that in Taos has been shared by so many? There must be more than fifty people acting on my behalf. In Wisconsin, I would not have the tribe of healers at my side, presiding over my physical and spiritual well-being, committed to carrying me through this atrocity. Taos is where I have the kind of holistic support I need, and my family is not able to give this particular kind of support. I'm leaning heavily toward Taos, but that leaves me far from family. There seems to be a never-ending division in my heart. I see no way to have it all and ultimately choose to go home for Christmas, looking for answers that cannot be found.

The visit is weighted with unrehearsed lines; no one in my family has ever been sick like this before. Communication, tested by the cancer and fueled by love, is raw. I feel awkward in the new role I've been forced into. I keep wanting to make it better, but I cannot; I want some one else to make it better, but they cannot either—not for me or, it seems, for themselves. We are a family in a dramatic play, in which the opening scene portends a tragedy and no one knows the ending. As I retreat to my room to rest and apply ointments to the burns, I feel like a wounded hound wanting to crawl off and die alone, so there will be no witness.

Finally, it's time to go back to Taos. In the car, as one of my brothers, Steve, drives us to the airport, a panic rises in me—a pull to stay—the innocent little girl inside me wanting to hear her mother's voice waking me from this nightmare. But this is real, and I resolve to return to my home in Taos. Even in this decision I do not feel safe, because honestly, I do not feel safe anywhere.

When we get to the airport, there's talk of a storm in Dallas, where we're scheduled to catch our connecting flight. Heavy winds, the loudspeaker says. On the plane, Tracy and I settle into our seats with apprehension. As the plane gathers speed and skitters into flight, it makes its leap of faith into open space with absolute conviction but hurtling toward an uncertain destination. A familiar feeling...

While we're in the air, the weather in Dallas gets worse and we're redirected to Kansas, where I lie on the floor of the bathroom for most of the layover. There, under the sickly fluorescent light of the ladies' room, is a woman who's on her own in a wheelchair, skeletal and very sick, drowning in a black leather jacket better suited to a linebacker. I suspect she has cancer.

My heart is breaking as she retches in the closed stall next to me. The plane is waiting for us, while she somehow gathers her strength to board. I want to grab hold of her in our sisterhood, to feel our thin, bony limbs rub against one another, to sob in unison without words over what each of us knows about the other. If I can hold up my own body I'll be able to reach out to her as she passes me, but I don't have the strength. Our eyes meet as she wheels past me. She is a reflection of me. I can feel her willpower, struggling to fight the illness, to travel to the place that will either heal the cancer or kill her. The force of her determination to live drowns out the seductive call of surrender and death. After eight hours in this cramped purgatory, we eventually board a plane to Dallas. Tracy and I are relieved, grateful to finally be on our way home.

We arrive in Dallas to the chaos that has been playing out all day and into the night. There are no flights out for days, no hotel rooms for fifty miles, and Tracy, try as she might, cannot find anyone to come to our aid. Everyone is in survival mode—on the phone, in lines that lead nowhere, angry—and a panic hangs in the air as I lay on the airport floor. Tracy pulls from her own resources to figure out a few options. After a 3 a.m. consultation with my brother Gil, we decide to get a rental car and drive home, or at least to a hotel. After ever more hours of lying on the floor, while Tracy stands in line, we secure a car. But Tracy is not old enough to drive a rental car, so, as absurd as it seems, I decide that I will drive us out of Dallas.

On loads of morphine and pain meds, I make it out to the highway and realize that my eyes can't bring the blurred lines on the road into focus. I'm not able to read the signs, it's raining lightly, and we're alone on this dark stretch. I look over at Tracy. "You're going to have to be my eyes," I say. "You tell me where I am on the road, and somehow we'll do this together."

I'm quite sure I've never seen this particular expression on my daughter's face before. She has been holding in her fear and concern for me for months, and now we've been thrown into a hell she never imagined. She has been brave until now, but it looks like she might crack—no words come from her mouth, but some form of agreement is made. Hours later, in the early dawn, we come upon a motel and sleep like the dead, straight through until checkout time. Our gears slowly grind back into motion. We agree to take it slow on the back roads, and Tracy will drive us the rest of the way home. We head for New Mexico, feeling like we've escaped the worst of it.

As we near the border, it's snowing. Unbelievably, it gets worse, and we find out that I-40 is closed down, along with all the side roads we had planned to take. We begin to look for a place to sleep in Amarillo, but once again, the masses have come before us. The cars are collectively pinned against the wall of snow, stopping all forward movement. We cannot find a room anywhere, at any price. It looks like we'll have to sleep in the rental car. We're wondering where to buy sleeping bags, when we decide to try one more motel. The woman at the front desk says there's no vacancy. I can't envision how we look to outsiders, but it must be desperate. Her husband comes up from behind her and says something about a room — one in no condition to rent. What do we care? "We'll take it," I manage to say.

With the gratitude of Mother Mary urgently seeking a place to unburden the life within her, we move into the cold, unready room. To us it looks like a palace.

Our luggage is on its way to who-knows-where, so we need supplies. I drive us to buy hats, pajamas, anything that can make us feel normal, warm and not in crisis. Tracy buys blue fingernail polish and soft pajamas with hearts on them. I go to the pharmacy. The nail polish will feed the Soul, but I can't get narcotics at an out-of-state pharmacy. I'm going to be in severe pain without them, and I'm starting to feel punished. I don't understand what's happening here. Why did I go home? Why didn't I just stay in Taos?

Every decision I make, every direction I go, seems the wrong one. I want to find peace. I want to rest...I want to be forgiven.

⋇

You will have to forgive me, God
I am not a saint
I see full well the arrogance with which I have built my
    sand castle
And defended it with my brazen wants
I tried not to, really I did
But it was so powerful to adore my body, to pay no heed to
    the passing of time
And to drift lazily like a wealthy princess in my dream castle.
With one swift movement of your grace you washed away
    all but
A few specks of sand
Was this a gift or a cruel misunderstanding on my part?
For I don't know how to change water into wine or walk on
    water or to...
Please forgive me
Be entirely consumed by your love

...I have no other choice than to surrender to your will
But you must remember one thing God
I am no saint

⋇

As we settle into our room in Amarillo, we learn that the storm is predicted to continue for almost a week. We have food delivered to the room and pee in the bathtub when the toilet won't flush, passing time any way we can. Tracy takes photos of the crystal-covered limbs outside the window. I make do with mixing the liquid morphine with Tylenol for pain until, on the third day of a six-day stay, I meet the woman from the front desk out in the hall. She reveals that she has just gone through breast cancer and has extra pain medications she can give me.

Perhaps there *is* a God.

We've been making calls from Tracy's cell phone, trying to figure out what to do, as the weather breaks slightly. Someone suggests I call the airline and ask them to help us. As I unravel our tale over the phone, the airline responds with immediate support. They can get us to Denver then on to Albuquerque, where we arrange with a friend, Cathy, to pick me up and get me home, while Tracy will head back to California.

Our last night in the motel is New Year's Eve. We're holding out hope that we'll be able to return the car, get to the airport, and make it home. It is bitter cold outside, and the heat has gone out with the electricity. With a tiny candle between us on the nightstand, the prospect of getting home renews our energy. Tracy humbly recounts stories from school. Some take on a confessional tone, with the emotion of eyes unseeing in the dark. Some of her stories make us laugh out loud in release, and our fears are transmuted into something like joy.

Just minutes before midnight, the TV lights up the room, and we watch as 2006 rolls over into 2007. Surely this will be an easier year.

I wonder where the wheelchair woman is and pray for her, and for myself.

The following day, we board a small plane to Denver. As we settle into our seats, Tracy takes hold of my hand and gives it a tender squeeze—our eyes meet as she extends reassurance and strength to me through her touch and smile. I feel enormous gratitude that we've had each other throughout this ordeal.

The way of a Soul is hard to understand. What appears on the surface is not the whole story...underneath it is the potential of the heart. Human beings have grave difficulties in the face of suffering; it wrenches the flow of blood and oxygen from the heart, leaving a lonely space.

But all that happens in a human life could not be otherwise. Nilama believes that by making the right choices, her suffering might diminish; but her suffering is only heightened by these burdens of choice. She thinks there is some place of safety that eludes her—and it is true, there is. But it is not on the Earth plane; it is in her heart, which is held within me, within the body of God.

Nilama and her daughter are ready for healing, for a connection that could not have happened without these events. God is compassionate but does not compromise the plan. Even though the Universe can appear cruel and perverse, the exhausting journey home together is the uncomfortable pressure required to squeeze the nectar of their love, beyond fear, in a realm of shared courage. These trials are necessary to widen their Souls; as with all tender moments, they are seared into pages of light for all time.

SEVEN

What is this veil between me and life? It is there, unseen yet tangible to me. When I look out through the veil into the world, I'm a stranger, and if I look into myself, I can get a glimpse of my wholeness. It grows daily. I am becoming shadow.

It is late in the night and I cry out at the loss of myself. I can't understand the path I'm on. How can this be happening to me? I can't remember the beginning of the journey anymore and certainly can't conceive of its ending. All my years of spiritual study seem to be failing me; my body is a field of pain wiping out the unconditional love I thought I held.

"I have a long way to go," I tell myself. I am in the kindergarten of consciousness. This pain humbles me like nothing ever has, and right now it brings me to this present moment. I want to avoid this moment. I don't want to feel what's happening in my body. I begin to make promises about what I would give, what I would do or not do, if this could just all go away—lifted from me by some miraculous action. The miracle, of course, depends on me deserving such a saintly gift. Old thoughts of not being good enough don't die as easily as the body. I embark on making myself good enough, and the passion with which the bargains are being made is surely honorable. Words form around the moment.

·⚬◦⚬·

I started to bargain with the Lord
Things I would do
Things I wouldn't do
Then I realized
Everything and anything I offered
Was already His

·⚬◦⚬·

I recall something I read in Stephen and Ondrea Levine's book *Who Dies?* It is one of the many books to which my lifetime fascination with death has drawn me. They write about pain, about its ability to abduct your senses and hold them hostage, and remind us that the energy we have in health may not be available in times of pain. What I remember goes something like this: "Imagine that you are sitting between two four-foot speakers that are blaring music you hate on high volume. That is how pain is when it steals your concentration, closes your heart, makes you small and incapable of the things you thought you would always be able to control. So, if you think that you can postpone meditating on your own death, think again."

I am not able to control this pain. I notice the harshness with which I judge myself, and I begin to understand his point. A measure of self-compassion bleeds into me, warm and noble. Until now, I have not embraced in myself that which I deem weak. I have tried to separate from myself, split into two, keep the frail me outside and only feel the part of me that can be strong. But this stance is not going to hold up under so much stress, and for the first time I truly begin to understand pain as a teacher.

I become aware of what's happening here. There's no need to become perfect to be loved. This entire body and being is made up of God. There is nothing about me, or in me, that is not God. There is no part that is undeserving. I am the love that made me. So how could I gamble against that which is, in its perfection, creating the very moment I'm experiencing? I have no bargaining power.

I start to see that all the parts of myself that I consider *me* are the creation of a masterful force, one that animates me, giving me breath and life. This life is a gift and this pain is a part of that gift; I receive it reluctantly, but I know it is mine. I have the choice to surrender to what is, which in this moment is a body in pain, or to suffer in resistance. I cannot get out of this body. I cannot barter with the Universe. I can only lie down in the dark, witness myself, be curious, not become the pain, and see the truth in the moment.

I recall the voice of my Soul (I began hearing it just a few weeks back), which told me: *This is what you came for.* I feel light and free. I surrender. That is all. Thy will be done.

∞

Everything that a human being has witnessed, created or shared with another is accumulated and stored as a future resource, a message to be unearthed at the proper time and place. Never doubt that there is a synchronicity to all the intricate workings of a life.

What is passed by without much thought may be the very thing that surfaces in a time of true need, perhaps as a string of newly gathered thoughts, or as words retrieved from another. Only then do I come to Nilama with pieces of her life reflected upon the light of her being, love demonstrating that she is in this world but not of it, and the truth that the life she views as "hers" belongs to the ages of the Universe.

EIGHT

The original date of the surgery has been postponed by ten days due to the fact that I took Arnica Montana, a homeopathic remedy for shock, which I am in (though I don't yet recognize the symptoms in myself).

The day before that scheduled surgery, I find out that the doctors are going to remove not only part of my rectum but the entire organ — a forty percent better chance of cure, the surgeon says. This is yet another hurdle I have no ability to leap. My friend Jean helps me complete a day of tests to prepare for the surgery. I'm exhausted and in a wheelchair, in the final conversation with a nurse, when it comes up that I took Arnica.

That evening in the hotel room, while reluctantly but obediently preparing my bowels, I get a call from my surgeon telling me that he is canceling the surgery. All of Jean's efforts and logic are wasted. I tell him that if I was in Europe, they would *want* me to take Arnica! But nothing will sway him. This changes all the plans Jean and I made; we begin again, to piece together a new plan of action. I have no idea how to name what I feel. There is anger, fear, relief...maybe it's a sign that God doesn't want me to do this.

My parents fly in to be with me for the postponed surgery. They are possibly as done in as I am. My father's unstable heart seems to be giving him trouble, and I call my brother Gil to see if he will come and support me through the surgery, as it appears that Mom may be taking care of Dad, and that leaves no one to take care of me. He drives the ten hours from Arizona to be here for me in time for the new surgery date. One of my many heroes.

I have plenty of time to doubt that this is the right decision.

For some reason, knowing that Farrah Fawcett is going through third-stage rectal cancer at the same time I am is a comfort. As my parents and I sit together in my living room, watching the news, they report that Farrah has chosen not to have her rectum removed. "If Farrah Fawcett doesn't have to have *her* rectum removed, why do I?" I demand of my parents, who are sitting side by side on the couch. I have learned that these two know how to stick together in life, and they look at me with what feels like one concerned face.

I am pacing the floor, stomping about like a petulant child. I'm sure that I'm making a bad choice. I want out. Out of all of it. My poor body! How will it keep taking these blows? I want to live. I want to feel sure about something —anything—in my life again. I tell them I've changed my mind. If Farrah has found a way to not remove her rectum, then I can too. I know my parents are saying something to me but I can't let the language into my brain. I cannot hear over my agitated movements, fearing that if I stop I'll have to go back to my old plan—or worse, disintegrate into tiny, shattered remnants of myself. Maybe if I can just move fast enough I can escape.

Finally fatigued, sitting there on the couch with my parents, I admit that I must do this surgery. Something is making me relent, and I don't know what it is. I feel as tired as I've ever felt in my life. I have no fight left in me for refusal.

.⠿⠿.

The tiny sharp slivers of silver lay on the cold brick
Like frozen scraps of stars
A spark and a blaze of blue heat entombs one speck of
      unsuspecting metal
The fire immediately puddles the hardness
Nothing is left to distinguish the form it once was

(Does it cry out... Can I bear this losing myself?)
The fire remains steady, unrelenting
Chaos ensues

.⠿⠿.

As Nilama's Soul, I am witness. I am her own self turned inward. Our shared home is fragile, and I, too, must endure this transmutation. I have no words of comfort for her at this moment. No language can describe what is to come. There is only this: God is merciful and just.

NINE

There is something coursing through my blood
It is what makes the cells divide, the DNA split and
The mitochondria produce energy
It is primal, ancient and timeless
It does not require me to notice it or acknowledge it
It is there whether I am asleep or awake
Dancing drunk with joy or pierced by grief
Filled with light or with engineered drugs that
Make me appear dead to the surgeon's knife
But it is alive
Cruising the golden pathways of life within me
And it has a voice
I can hear it even from the void I am in
It gives me the command that rules the Universe
So simple, so surprising

You are the love of God
Breathe

I am in the recovery room. The eight-hour surgery is over.
I am not yet awake. I am floating in some void—nothing

to report from the blackness. Until I hear the words *"You are the love of God—BREATHE!"* Was I thinking that I would *not* breathe? I don't know the answer to this, but with an in-breath, air enters my hungry lungs and my eyes open in the recovery room. Standing beside me, with uneasy grins on their faces, are my parents, my brother, and the surgeon. It's all very surreal. My father's phone rings and it's another one of my brothers, Mike, who lives in France. I hear him through the fog asking me how I am. I respond with something about drinking margaritas. Strange answer, but it lightens the weight I sense in the room.

They tell me I have a strong heart, and my vital signs are so good I do not have to be in the ICU ward.

Late that night, my doctor tells me there's been a miracle. The biopsy reveals that the cancer has not spread as far as they had thought, and that all the boundaries are clear. They downgrade me to stage-two cancer. I recall the weekly prayer circle that the last group of massage students I taught has been doing for me. The master healers who have laid their hands on me. Native American sweat lodges held in my honor. The website Justin set up through which people from all parts of my life are sending blessings. The weekly letters from my sister in the same pile as a hundred others filled with love and good wishes. Prayers in the Buddhist, Catholic, Native American, and Hindu traditions —all for me. I even receive a letter from my Hindu teacher in India, sending her love to me and my family. I am held through this time in ways I could not have held myself. What great good fortune I have. I believe in the power of prayer and I know the news about the cancer should make me happy and grateful, but after the massive surgery I've just lived through, I don't have that self-possession.

I lie in a dark room because I cannot tolerate the light that wants to break through the window; it's too sharp, too revealing. My meditation shawl is covering me and the sacred chant I listened to through the surgery is set on repeat, the headphones directly streaming God's divine name into my mind. I want to stay in this cocoon, protected. I have no interest in seeing any more of the results than I already know.

As I look down toward my feet, bound in pumps to keep my blood flowing to prevent clots, my slight body is but a ripple in the bed covers. Tubes spring out of every orifice, and at the end of bruised arms, three drip lines crowd the tops of each of my hands. My belly has thirty-odd staples in a vertical pattern, and I feel a strange sensation, open and vulnerable, on the right side of my abdomen, where the ileostomy resides.

I feel nailed to the bed. Visions of Christ on the cross.

My surgeon has reluctantly agreed to give me some extremely strong pain medication for my high pain levels, but only for three days. After that I'll have to learn to endure it. He is a tough master.

I begin to move my arms up and down to the rhythm of the steadiest breath I can manage, and since I'm in the right position, I practice *shavasana* — corpse pose in hatha yoga. Throughout the week, as I learn to walk again, my brother catches me when I fall, my mother braids my greasy hair as she did when I was a child, and on Valentine's Day she brings in red-paper hearts and a sign that says "Hug Me."

When the pain becomes unbearable, I ask the interns to tell me stories of their lives. I hear about camping trips and upcoming marriages. The normal lives of others brings me some peace. My friend Shankari has tucked into my bag a bottle of essential oil, called Joy, and I dowse myself with it daily until the nurses say they can smell it down the hall. No problem though, they say; it uplifts the entire floor. An East Indian intern tells me he always looks forward to coming into my room. He says it is *clean.*

I have plenty of time to contemplate the words I heard in the recovery room, *"You are the love of God —*
BREATHE," but they have no solid place to land. If only I could live the rest of my life with the truth of these words, what a life I would lead. These ideas float freely in me. If before this I was shadow, now I am mist.

∞

I love Nilama... and the people who come to aid and comfort her. Some make her laugh and some make her cry. Some, like her surgeon, leave her wounded by their abrasiveness, and from so many others she receives deep, unconditional love. In time, a compassion will be unveiled for all the beings who join Nilama on her journey, each carefully carved into the earthen vessel of life for everyone's benefit.

Nilama is learning to see through eyes of equanimity, to look beyond the borders of dissonant words, violent deeds, and skin.

TEN

I have to pee. I have to make it to my bathroom. As I step into the dawn light of the familiar room of my home, I notice something reflected in the full-length mirror. I stare, but I don't know what I'm looking at. For some time I stand in wonder as to what it could be. Then I realize it's *me*. I don't know if I'm more shocked by the fact that I don't recognize myself or by the sight I behold before me.

How could this be me? My ribcage and hips and knees are nearly exposed bone. No meaty flesh covers my skeleton, no hair curls from translucent skin, no breasts bulge behind nipples. And there's a clear plastic bag hanging from my abdomen, full of my own excrement. Images of Nazi concentration camp prisoners float through my vision. I lose breath; I lose the moment. Then I think, *this is what I will look like when I'm dead.*

I want to remember this moment. I look closer, studying every detail. As I take in the texture, color and shape of the cut traversing my midline, I think this is one of the few identifying marks that will distinguish me at the morgue.

I am engaged with my death-body; the intimacy makes my mind swoon. I deem this my Buddhist moment.

The necessity of loss
It strips me down
Down to the undertow of unbreathable space
So that I can learn to breathe the water again
To be taken back home
To where I began
So I can begin again

ELEVEN

Obsessed with putting on weight before the reversal of the ileostomy, I'm eating everything in sight. I've continued on a clean Ayurvedic diet — the practice of food as medicine. But I know this menu won't put on the pounds necessary for the next round of torment. So I add blueberry muffins, pancakes with butter and syrup, chocolate cake, ice cream. My friend John has me eating lamb chops and steaks; food I have not touched for years, I now chew with abandon, giving myself full permission.

I am not judging the intuition to eat whatever my body craves. But the home healthcare nurse is concerned that I may be setting myself up for failure. She's never seen a person with an ileostomy put on much weight. I'm determined to gain a pound a week, which would bring me to 115 pounds by the time of the surgery. During every visit, after she inspects the ileostomy, she reluctantly brings in the scale to record my progress, as I insist, and at every visit I've put on weight.

My new diet makes some of my friends nervous: doesn't sugar feed cancer? But Sandy, one of my holistic doctors, supports me completely, and gives me rose-petal jam to ease my heart.

I'm driving again, doing yoga, and making plans to go back to work. I see the light at the end of the tunnel with this cancer thing. My life awaits me, and I am anxious to get back to what I love.

I feel a sense of triumph. I'm making it through.

The surgeon says the reversal procedure is no big deal, not to worry, some people even go home the same day. Our relationship has been tense, communication almost non-existent, and I have involved patient advocacy due to his unreasonable demands. I'm relieved that after this last procedure, he won't figure as prominently in my care. But he's a brilliant surgeon, so I practice conciliation, more out of weakness than strength, because I'm honestly afraid of him.

He holds the knife. He holds my life.

∞

Sometimes in life it is necessary to let go and trust your intuition.

TWELVE

It's the day after the ileostomy reversal, and things are not going well. I was up all night with interns who finally, after many tries, got a baby catheter inserted so my bladder could drain. It was an extremely painful process, one that left me emotional and weak, the drain for my bladder adding to the trauma of the reversal.

The surgeon enters my room midmorning. He casually leans against the wall, at the greatest distance from me. He distills the circumstances down to the fact that I am ready to leave the hospital. After about twenty minutes of lecture and abuse in front of five interns, as I reject the notion that I am well enough to leave, and in tears, he tells me that someone will not get their surgery today if I do not give up my bed. He is nonchalant about the state I am in, and he impassively states that he is releasing me from the hospital, as is, catheter and all. In his view, I am certainly able to take care of these medical appendages myself at home.

After he leaves the room, one of the interns comes to my bedside and offers her sincere apology for the way I was treated, and another takes my hand and says, "I know this is hard, but if you don't do as the surgeon says, you'll have to contend with his wrath." I am angry and exhausted and in full loathing of this man who calls himself a healer. I never imagined that in the weakest moments of my life I would be treated with such disdain.

I'm throwing my things together to leave as the nurse comes in. "What do you think you're doing?" she demands as she walks into my room. "I'm leaving!" I yell back at her, barely able to stand without leaning on the bed. I explain that the surgeon has insisted I leave the hospital. The story is fueled by the fact I have been through this before with him. Only five days after my first surgery, the one in which he had removed my rectum, he gave orders for me to be released from the hospital. It had been six o'clock at night, midwinter, and my parents had walked from the motel to the hospital, so we didn't have a car. Responding to this man's domineering nature, the situation had been handled nervously by the attending surgeon on my case. With my pain level rising at the prospect of being forced to do the impossible task of leaving at a moment's notice, it had been determined that I stay. Besides, they can't make you leave the hospital if you don't have a means of transportation.

Not the least bit daunted by the surgeon's question-able orders, the nurse gets me back into bed, insisting that I stay. "People stay as long as five days with a reversal. You haven't even passed gas or had a bowel movement yet and we're responsible for your recovery." Then she calls patient advocacy.

⧜

Abused power has gnarly age-old roots wrapped tightly around
underground boulders, gripping ancient artifacts left behind by
hands of the past. They seek the freedom of clear rivers in lost, buried
caverns. They are born of humiliations passed on and seared into
hearts by the horrors of those who came before them. Unchecked,
they wreak havoc above ground and disperse their pain.

This is the beginning of a cruel twist of fate. Even I, the
Soul, cannot always see the benefit of such events, but I know that
the Dark Goddess is now in charge. Together we will learn what this
fearless Goddess has in mind. I will not relinquish my duty to usher
Nilama through this time, but I am no match for the great Gods.
In all light, there is the Goddess of the dark; this unity of opposites
composes the web of the Universe. Tough love is never easy, but it
yields compassion.

❧

What is there to say about a Goddess whose
Love is so complete that she would cut off your head so
    you could
Finally get the truth of who you are and what you are doing
    on this
Beautiful Earth?
She doesn't hesitate at pain
She won't flinch an inch at your deep suffering
You can beg for your life as you know it to return and
Make promises that you could never humanly keep

She smiles back at you and although her eyes fill to the brim
To see you laid to the bottom of your tomb
She does not give way

Even if it has been years in the darkness
Time means nothing to her
Age means nothing to her
What she holds dearest is that you return to God
Her fearless love is the sweet call home

⁘ ⸙ ⁘

THIRTEEN

Tracy has left, having cared for me for three days after the ileostomy reversal. I am alone in the house for a few days until my parents arrive. My bowels are in a state of constant complaint. Day and night, every half hour or so, I'm in the bathroom. I need sleep. I need to feel better. I call the surgeon's office and get his head nurse. I describe what's happening and her response is a question that makes me feel marginalized and judged. She asks, "Well, what herbs have you been taking?" I hang up the phone, not able to understand what just happened. I know something is wrong but I don't know what it is.

I have no fever, but I'm deteriorating. I'm bodiless and lost. They told me this was going to be easy. My parents arrive, once again, from Wisconsin and are gravely concerned. I have a doctor's appointment tomorrow. Perhaps he can determine what's going on.

I've been in varying levels of constant pain for a year. I can't take it any more. My spirit is desiccated and I have no more fight in me. I'm even sicker than at the height of chemo and radiation and burns. For too long I haven't been able to sleep, and the despair I feel at this moment is immeasurable. Life is not supposed to be like this. All I can think about is getting out of pain. I can take no more of it.

·⤮⤮·

I moved as if asleep
I gathered my allies for the moment
Morphine, lortab, lorazepam
They were the pathway to freedom
Freedom from this body
It would be so easy ... just ... swallow

·⤮⤮·

I hold an overdose in the palm of my hand. Moonlight crosses the darkness of my room. I'm taking an inventory of the people in my life. I know this would be devastating to my parents, who are sleeping in the next room, but I convince myself they could survive it, along with my brothers and sister. I believe that all the people who love me would understand the pain I'm in and give me their blessings. Clearly the pain I'm in right now far outweighs the pain they would feel if I were gone. I believe I'm choosing a clean solution to the problem. I don't want to live anymore.

·⤮⤮·

...Then my heart screamed
What about *her?*
The Soul you carried for nine months
Your first, your only
And I saw her face
And I heard her laugh
And I remembered the feel of her at my breast

Would the pain I inflict on her be greater than mine in
    this moment?
There is no answer for this
There is only the witness of the suffering of the world
Of legless beggars on trains
Of mothers holding dying hungry children
Of being eaten alive by life itself
If not for them, then for her
For she is the world

               ⸙

Love pours through the vessel of my heart at the
sound and vision of my daughter. It is a powerful force
that stops me cold—Tracy's laughter and smile. I cannot
leave her alone in the world. We have so much to share
yet, so much I want to witness of her budding life. I cannot
put the pills into my mouth and wash them down with the
liquid morphine. I want the pain to stop; I long for relief.
I pause, wishing I could end this misery, but because of
Tracy, I know I will not do it.

               ⸙

Save me from my small self
The one that begs for mercy not believing God hears
Let me fall to my knees with a Heart and Soul
Raw from misunderstanding and
Be held in the arms of angels
That assure me that I can understand
I am truth
I am pure light

I am pure love
And not give in to death's tricks any more…
Death will have to do his own work

I wake my mother, empty the pills from my hands into hers, and tell her to hide all the drugs in the house. She instantly gathers everything, even the vitamins, understanding well the gravity of the moment. In dim light, my parents and I sit on the edge of my bed; through tears and confusion, I confess my not wanting to live anymore. This gruesome desire to no longer exist combines mysteriously with the powerful love I feel inside me and my desperation to live. I just don't know how to take the next step. If once I was a shadow, then mist, now I am nothingness. I am empty. I have pleaded with God, to no avail, to end the pain. Instead, like battery acid on an open wound, the situation becomes worse than ever. What is this love that can stop me from ending my life but refuses to gift me release from the pain?

My parents and I sit together for a long time. Silence swirls with spare words of love.

I have taken up full residence in Nilama's heart. I employed her connection to her daughter to deliver the only thing that matters: love. I will stoke a fire here, in her heart, that will burn her to the ground, creating the very ash with which the Dark Goddess will anoint her body and then take her to her spiritual death.

FOURTEEN

The next day, my fever spikes at the doctor's office twenty miles from Taos. The look on the nurse's face is nothing compared to my mother's as she looks at the thermometer. Due to my "suicide attempt" last night (although I contemplated it, I did *not* take the pills), professional ethics dictate that I wait to see the psychologist. When the doctor sees my spiking temperature, though, he forgoes protocol and sends us to the emergency room back in Taos. My father drives as I lie in the backseat of my pickup. My mother rides shotgun, and no one says anything. I'm freezing to death and feel like I'm dying, which it appears is everyone's fear at the moment. There must be an infection somewhere in my body.

Back in the hospital, I apologize to the nurse every time she comes in to clean up the puddle of feces in which I lie. She is as gracious about it as she might be handing me a bouquet of flowers for my troubles. Shivering from cold, I'm taken for tests. After hours of pursuing the problem, drugs administered, I am stabilized. The initial plan of transporting me to Albuquerque in a Flight for Life helicopter is canceled, and I am carried to my next destination in an ambulance. Not that I register it at the time, but this leaves my seventy-nine-year-old parents in quite a jumble.

The ambulance ride is a blur. Miraculously I make it to the next hospital. I am not tracking well, but from what I gather there is a microscopic hole in one of the internal stitches, allowing leakage from my bowels into my abdomen. I am taken to a scanner so they can run a tube through my backside into the abscess and drain the infection, while antibiotics are intravenously entering my bloodstream to save my life.

I am angry. Did I live through chemo, radiation, and major surgery just to die of an infection? The absurdity of this thought courses through me. Too much has happened in a condensed time frame. I see myself deep in a shadowy forest, unable to discern leaves from branches or light from dark, or penetrate the tangled woods to open a ray of sunlight to warm me. The aftereffects of the near suicide leave me grasping for an unseen heat, the warmth of love's wishes — and now this life might be taken from me.

It's a strange thought in these circumstances, but I'm glad to have been so adamant about putting on weight, because this infection is already eating precious pounds off my frame. I will need everything my tiny body can muster to ride this through.

When I finally stabilize, I am released from the hospital and find myself back at home, but honestly I don't remember how I got here.

My parents leave; they have arranged for a longtime friend, Jennie, to come from Wisconsin to be with me. I am alone until Jennie is scheduled to come in about two weeks. Friends must be coming by and bringing me food, checking on me, because I'm bedridden once again and cannot drive.

My nervous system is overwhelmed, and the traumas continue to accumulate. I have very little recollection now of my day-to-day existence through this stretch of time, only that there is aliveness percolating in me that I can only call Grace, infusing into the bone marrow, producing blood, feeding my tender heart, making it beat.

Ah...walking the razor's edge, so sharp and fine. It is the holiest of times: on one side, human life; and on the other, the absolution of the spirit—the weight of the body cutting against the blade and a gradual education about the necessity of loss, while humans balance life against death. Either will suffice, but for now, life will be the outcome. This passage will once again be laid before Nilama as it will for all humans, and then there will be only one option. Freedom.

FIFTEEN

The infection is winning. I can feel it taking over my body again. Jennie will be here in hours, but I know this dangerous predator and cannot wait; it's moving fast in me. I call friends, one of whom (another Jenny) leaves work to come get me, and I'm back in the emergency room.

It seems impossible, but I'm even sicker than I was two weeks ago.

I've lost all the precious weight I worked so hard to put on. I'm freezing, my teeth chattering and my body shaking. A fever is raging though me, trying to kill the invader. The doctors want to do tests and I can't figure out how they can get a clear picture with all the shaking I'm doing under layers of heated blankets. I opt to move forward with the tests, not because I'm making any kind of decision, but because it never occurs to me to say anything—least of all, *no*. The incoherence of the illness and the morphine take me to a place where I'm unaware that I'm a person in a body. I can witness the scene unfolding around me, but I'm not engaged in it.

The ER doctor is sitting beside me, holding my hand. I know he's telling me what's going on with my body, but all I notice is the compassion in his voice and the gentleness with which he touches me. It seems there's a spiritual warmth glowing in him and generously entering me, moving me to participate by the supreme softness he exudes. I tell him that if there's anything I can do to help them help me, they should let me know. Jennie and Jenny hold watch at the end of the bed, until Jenny goes out into the hall with the doctor. As I find out only later, he tells her he thinks I am dying, and there's nothing more they can do. We'll have to wait and see.

But I'm not having thoughts of death. Blessedly, I find myself in a state of rapture. I can touch the love in the room — see the divine elegance of each person around me — and I'm basking in it. I am no longer aware of being cold and afraid, or that I'm in a hospital bed. I feel an ease that is so close to who I am that it has no defining properties; it renders me free and full of love, but even these words do no justice to where I find myself. It would never have occurred to me that this could be a precursor to death. It simply feels like where I've always longed to be. As I look at the faces of the these two women, my guardian angels, that's exactly what I see: angels in human form, light shining through them into me, and I am in total peace. I'm thinking, "My God, they are beautiful; *we* are all so beautiful."

I am in an ambulance again. I see the Dark Goddess, Kali, dancing around me. Blood is dripping from her tongue; the heads and arms that adorn her body swing to the wild dance that taunts my existence. I become aware of how I keep clinging to my past self, my old life — and from this place, that life seems centuries gone. Is this a hallucination or a visitation? No matter, I humbly relinquish my life to this Goddess.

"Take what you have come for," I say, as if my life is mine to give away. This life, with all its horrors and joys, belongs to the Lord who created it, and when He wishes the return of His vessel, The Mother will call her child home. I believe the time of my death is set by the Divine unfolding of Shiva and Shakti, the royal creators, destroyers, and sustaining governors of all life. Nothing I have contrived to sway the outcome of this moment matters. I am bound to my Soul and left to the benevolence of this Dark Goddess.

Nilama has remembered that the moment of birth is set in time, as is the moment of death. This is not the time of her physical death, but of teachings to be implanted in her heart for the benefit of her future awakening. Death is not a failure, and living is not a reward. It is as it shall be. All life is eternal, and within that truth there can be no death. The surrender of the borrowed body to the earth is my release. The freedom that can be glimpsed from the state in which Nilama finds herself is the final freedom for us all; to hold this particular freedom is the duty of death, until we rise again to create and play within the dance of the Divine Wonder.

Nilama will always remember this time of her awakening and believe that it has been a preview of her final ascent into the arms of God. It will leave Nilama ghostlike in the world and curious about the mysteries she has lived through. But her work is not finished on this planet. As she struggles to fill in her new shape, she will say to friends, "Dying is easy; it is living that is hard."

꧁

I tell you this
In my final days do not worry so about my body, the pain,
    the suffering
I beg you
I implore you
Help me remember who I am
Take me deep into the landscape within
Open the windows of my Soul with your eyes
That love may pour forth
Stir the pool of my voice so that only sacred mantras fill
    the air
Caress the air so that my ears only hear the angels calling
    me near
Carry my heart with your heart into the vast expanse
    of eternity
I swear to you that in this way we will never never be apart
I will dance on your lips
Vibrate the wheels of life within you and
Draw you constantly into devotion
And so it will be
Blood of my blood
Womb of my womb
That we will glide the star streams together
and rest in the palm of God

꧁

SIXTEEN

This last week in the Albuquerque hospital has been undeniably strange. They gave my bed away while I was en route from Taos. I'm being held in a hallway, with the ambulance workers at my side assuring me they won't leave until I'm safely in a room — saints, each of them. These months have brought to my bedside opposing angels — some holding my life with compassion and grace, going out of their way to aid in my healing; others seeming not even to see me as a living, breathing person.

Once back in a proper room, they refuse me Tylenol for the fever. The surgeon has commanded that no one do anything until he comes out of surgery. The residents' hands appear tied. Jennie is pacing the room like a mama bear — this is crazy! She has witnessed me through this illness, struggling to stay alive, and now they're refusing me the very thing I need to help me live? I have a fever of 105, I'm packed in ice, and I need medicine. It turns out that the tube inserted in my body to drain away the infection is too small to do the job.

Jennie takes matters into her own hands and goes down to the gift shop to buy Tylenol. While she's gone, two resident doctors enter my room, and I complain about what's going on. One looks directly at me and states, "You

can leave if you don't like the care you're getting here."
Really? I just spent the entire night in emergency rooms,
ambulances and hallways, in the arms of death, and by
some miracle I have managed to hang on, only to be
reproached for speaking my mind? I can barely lift my
head, let alone walk out of here — and if I could I would,
quite pleased never to be in this place again. I'm angry and
silently curse this woman, along with the surgeon. Are they
actually trying to kill me? She has learned well from the
surgeon who is training her, I think.

Another clear case for patient advocacy, which I call
upon to govern on my behalf once again.

Finally, Tylenol has manifested and been administered. This lowers the fever, but I'm still very fragile. It's
impossible to imagine, in the light of everything that's
happened in the past year, that I'm still alive. I lie in the
hospital bed, a whisper of a human being, without a past,
a future, or anything that resembles who I once was. Some
friends visit throughout the week; Jennie sleeps in my
room and I have visions of her moving about, keeping me
safe, her keen eye ever watchful.

My life plans have now been thrown into the
sacramental fire with everything else. My new clean slate
has been reduced to ash. Soon, with this sacred emptiness
packed inside me, it will be time to leave the hospital and
go back to Taos.

"When we get you out of here," Jennie promises,
"I'm taking you home to Wisconsin and your parents.
You cannot do this alone anymore." This sounds like the
most sane idea I've heard in a long time. My entire being

relaxes at the thought of being completely cared for in the arms of my mother, to recover from the past year in my childhood home.

I close the door to my house in Taos after five days home from the hospital, without a thought or care as to the outcome of everything I know and own in the world. I am focused on larger matters, like taking the next breath. It is 7-7-7, the day gay marriage is legalized in California. I marvel at all the things going on in the world. Everything I could possibly imagine is happening to someone today. From the horror of war crimes against the innocent, to newborn babies' lips attaching for the first time to their mothers' full breasts. Life and death, joy and sorrow, suffering and celebration — what a fine line we all walk.

Jennie and I will be on an airplane soon. We're in a bathroom stall at the airport doing our best to clean the tube that is draining the infection from my body. We need sterile water to do this and evidently more space than we have. This soul sister and I first met in kindergarten. We grew up in the residue of the sixties, and, once we were both married, we shared in the experience of motherhood, always catching time by the tail and reuniting with ease. Today, we are like two young girls sharing a bathroom stall for the first time; it feels a bit dangerous and funny at the same time. We bump the walls, trying not to drop anything precious into the open toilet, and as she ever-so-motherly presses the liquid through the catheter to clean the life-saving tube, I feel a bond with this woman well beyond the moment. A tear fills the corner of my eye as I take in this familiar feeling of connection that has been enlarged by all the acts of tenderness, offered by so many, throughout the past year; this small act, I realize, along with all the others, is the act of Love.

After the huge effort to get this wafer-thin body on the plane, I finally settle into a middle seat. I am exhausted and relieved; we did it, we got me to this place. Now, maybe, if the Goddess would take some pity, I can get some rest.

My brother Steve and his children, along with my parents, will pick me up at the other end of the trip. The seat next to me is empty. I gratefully take up the extra space and say a prayer of gratitude to the extra-seat-next-to-you-on-the-plane Goddess. Jennie has the window seat. I release a long breath and close my eyes.

"You don't look well enough to be on this plane!" I hear the rather stern tone in the stewardess's voice and realize it's directed at me. This is true, but there's no way I'm getting off this plane. Before I can muster the strength to speak, Jennie replies for me, meeting the intensity of the stewardess: "She's with me and she's just fine!"

I try to imagine how I appear to those around me. As I manage the difficult but necessary trips to the bathroom, people avert their eyes from mine, choosing to make me invisible. For most, I'm just too much to witness on a sunny summer July day.

A paper-napkin note with a business card wrapped inside it slips through from the seat behind me. It says, "My wife says I give a very good foot massage. They help her sleep." Jennie and I peer over the seat to find a man traveling with his young son, who is practicing his reading skills out loud. The outpouring of warmth from this man's face could melt any heart. I do not opt for a foot massage, but open myself to conversation. He has just recently come from helping his mother in her dying process and understands all too well what I'm going through. He encourages me to stay strong. I can make it through this, he says.

I find love in most unexpected places.

∞

With this act of surrender, returning to her childhood home, Nilama is removed from the Master's anvil. The alchemy has transpired, and now she will have the freedom to find the purpose of her experience with cancer. As the Creator ecstatically lowers the flame, Nilama's will returns and she can now begin to inhabit her new expression. Will she hear The Call? Will she take heed of the responsibility now placed in her path?

Like all children of God, Nilama will sometimes forget the power of her experience; then, because of Grace, she will remember again to cherish the gifts with greater intention. Nilama will carry this weight of physical limitation and spiritual paradox. These mysteries—which leave humans questioning how and why such horrors exist—belong to her, as do all the experiences of her life. The answer so many seek as to "why" is unnecessary. The life that Nilama lives is the one and only expression of her that could make this journey this way.

This journey, in its entirety, is the gift of the Sacred, and although her particular experience belongs only to her, all transformations belong to the Soul of the Universe, within which we all reside together. God and Goddess, all the saints, and the sweet exhalation that enlivens the human heart, are as close as our own breath. So breathe, Dear Ones. Breathe in the pain and the joy, and know that you are made of stardust, and that every particle of your being is a Universe unto itself.

❦

Oh! The sweet release of a tear
As the well of the eye fills
And one tiny, thin line slowly slides down the cheek
Like a trickle of water that flows on the parched desert floor
Its message the account of its precious journey…
"Contained in the interior vastness, you are all that you
　　　encounter. Every cell a Universe of such beauty it
　　　cannot be described. Do not doubt that you are that
　　　beauty. You are the thirsty desert floor, the urgent
　　　flower, the salty mineral and the hesitant water. So let
　　　them come, Dear One. Let them cover the ground of
　　　your body, for they are from the womb of the Mother,
　　　and where they touch, new life will grow."

❦

SEVENTEEN

Carried in the arms of a friend
I was a child again
Back to the room where my dreams began
The man and woman who bore me
Silently awaiting the outcome of my life

I spend the next year in my parents' home, recovering, rebuilding, and connecting to my parents in their world. It's a gift to get this kind of time with them at this stage of their lives; to be in their quiet, everyday routine settles my nervous system. I have no responsibility to anything or anyone but myself, and my healing.

I hardly remember these first weeks and months. They are torture, and I don't feel much like living. I find it impossible to sleep with my bowels so inflamed and in such constant motion. I feel wasted away, deprived of life; I cry daily, housed in depression. How long can a person in my condition go without sleep? There is no answer to this, and we fall into a sort of orderly chaos, taking each day as it comes. My mother changes my bed sheets while I bathe, cooks my meals, and tends to my emotional trauma. Dad's job is to make me smile. The fact that my parents are in good health and take me into my childhood home with open arms is a fortunate blessing that does not go unnoticed.

One night, my brother Dan is having dinner with us. Mom's chicken-noodle soup steams in bowls on the table. But I feel like I'm going to throw up, and the combined work of sitting upright at the table and lifting the spoon to my mouth overwhelms me. With illness robbing me of all inhibitions, I burst into tears and my head falls to the table, cushioned ever so slightly by the tablecloth. I feel immensely tired and wish I had the courage to just die. I leave the dining room to retreat to the comfort and solitude of my bed. Dan quietly enters my room and, with the most tender act I can recall from him in my life, he gently places wandering hair behind the curve of my ear, while his soothing words of comfort reassure me.

Eventually, I get into the medical system in Wisconsin and meet with an oncologist, Dr. Junket. He is a dream come true. He has solutions to many of my pressing issues, and amazingly, as I sit with him, instead of getting up and holding the doorknob with a cursory "Anything else?" he stays seated, for two hours, and asks "What else?" His genuine consideration for me is evident in his tone and his compassionate gaze. This may seem like a small difference, but to those of you who have been here, you know it is massive. I'm able to unload fears, ask questions and be given time to think, without sensing that any of my concerns are unimportant or trivial, or that he could spring up and walk out of the room at any time. Together, we go into every detail I can come up with until the list is exhausted. His act of compassion, patience, and expertise has helped me turn the corner, heading me once again toward healing.

Back home on a cold, dark winter evening, with the sound of the furnace kicking in and rattling its warmth into the kitchen, Mom is washing the dinner dishes while I dry them. Familiar smells of childhood are in the house, and Dad is in the living room listening to jazz on the stereo. We are chatting lightly when I tell her this feels like a do-over. It's a complex statement that I know she doesn't fully understand, because I'm just beginning to grasp it myself. When I was born, there were three siblings who had died before me, and I feel a ghostly parallel experience between fifty years ago and now. The pain of my parents' past grief, and their wonderment around my survival, feels all too close. We have blood memory stored deep inside us, and I am privy to a view of my own karmic past and its connection to the present moment. Once again, it appears that I will live; I feel a fragile, fetal bond with my mother, and I'm offered a vision that gives me the opportunity to heal old, primal, prebirth fears. This may never have happened without the cancer, and strangely I am grateful for where I find myself.

In the spring, almost ten months into my stay with my parents, we're sitting at the breakfast table. I'm a bit frustrated with the conversation because it sounds like the same one we've been having since I arrived. Perhaps it's a good sign of my improved health to even notice this pattern, but my buttons are being pushed a bit, and my patience is thin. I'm wondering how I could be having such resistance to these two people. They have been through hell and back with me and yet here I am, overcome by my small emotions. What to do with these petty feelings?

As I look across the table into their faces, I mute the conversation, letting the past months of intimacy rise up, and I see two incredible people whom I love very much. Little pictures snipped from time remind me of their courage and the love they've shown me. We've had our troubles and our triumphs together, and perhaps these repeating conversations are the very ones I'll remember with humor when I'm no longer with them. I know I will miss them, cherish the early summer drives Dad took us on through Amish country to buy cheese, me slouched in the backseat doing my best to look out into the world; or Mom, getting so excited watching the Green Bay Packers, up on her feet shouting orders to the quarterback; and the quiet moments we had every afternoon at five o'clock when they had their evening cocktail and I drank herbal tea.

As Mom rises to clear the breakfast dishes from the table, I vow to remember and appreciate every detail about them. Tears form as I feel the release of frustration and embrace the love I have for them. These two people, whom I hold dear like no others in my life, have always accepted me. And although it's true they will probably never really understand me, I am their child, their daughter, and I know they love me.

∞

When healing occurs in one generation, it expands in time to the past, present and future generations in the ancestral lines. Time, a concept of the mind, is not linear; it knows no bounds and fills dimensions unimaginable by the human mind. By going home and receiving this nurturing care from her family, Nilama opens doors that once were left ajar. These insights connecting her past and present death experiences are of tremendous importance to her future healing and that of her family.

The act of receiving is very powerful and brings balance to life. Nilama, once out of balance, had placed herself more often in the position of the giver, which on one level kept her in control and not having to be vulnerable; but now she must trust others to be there for her when she needs them. The trauma that held back the bond of trust in her family at the time of her birth can now be witnessed. The cancer has resurrected the same scenario for everyone involved: They will each discover for themselves what part they played, or did not play. Most important for Nilama, it is no longer held in a dark prison of concealed grief.

Exposed to the light, unguarded, undefined emotions are released and set free.

Cancer has helped Nilama realize that the joy she felt in giving was reflected in the eyes and hearts of others. Now it's their chance to feel and receive that joy. Nilama can now better understand the delicate balance between giving and receiving that brings people together in shared trust and compassion. The human ability to show up consciously for one another in times of need is one of the true gifts bestowed by the Creator. For in this act, one may recognize the face of God in another.

EIGHTEEN

I give my parents a final hug in the driveway. My little car is stuffed with my most precious belongings, grabbed hastily in fleeing Taos almost a year ago. I feel somewhat numb, sad and not quite ready to return to Taos, but I'm determined to press myself into my own world again.

My brother Mike gives me lessons on his new Blackberry so I can respond to his secretary's calls while he drives me as far as Boulder, where I spend a week resting and rebuilding to be able to drive myself the final distance home.

My house, rented to a friend through the winter, seems to have missed me and patiently awaited my return. It offers me a place of repose — a time to rediscover who I might be at this juncture of healing. I move slowly in life now. I can manage one errand in a day, a couple of days a week. I keep my bed in the living room so I don't have to spread out too far in the house and fill space I haven't the energy to fill. The cocoon-like walls contain me and help me feel safe.

There are new levels of learning how to tend to myself with absurd care, and to uncover the mysteries of my foreign body. My heart, blackened by fire, requires persuasion to open again, to trust life and to heal, so I can once again be present with this precious life.

The world is moving so fast that I feel out of sync with everything around me. I no longer feel part of the intricate dealings of a material life. I am a ghost, stripped of identity, roaming the lives of others and wondering where I belong.

I have ample time to contemplate the way we humans consume Earth's material resources—and each other—at unprecedented speed.

When I was young, we had a telephone on the kitchen counter; we shared the line with our neighbors. They called it the party line. Although there was some pride in having such technology available to us, the phone did not join us at the dinner table, ride in the car with us, or accompany us to school. Now, as I watch from my encased world, I see how the cancer of the past few years has removed me from a technological explosion, leaving me behind and bewildered. I feel like an alien, unable to understand the recurrent talk of upgrading phones, computers, and iPads, all competing for our consumption. Everything I once knew is outdated.

I feel I must catch up, and I pressure myself to think about work and how to make money, so I can carve out my place in this fast-moving scenario. Then, depleted by the very thought of this, I get honest with myself and honor my embryonic pace in the world. I have to admit that, from where I sit, it looks like a feeding frenzy by piranhas held in raging waters that no part of me can dip into. It takes valuable energy just to keep my foot from getting caught in the whirlpool.

There is a longing in me to feel connected to the world again, but which world? What do I want to create with my life...what statement do I wish to make...with what voice? Do I have a solid enough identity to be in this world? The answer to these questions, for now, is no. I don't know what I want or who I have become or who I will be. The only word that comes to mind is *safe*. I want to feel safe. So I step back, breathe, and wonder at my existence and at the state of the world in which I now find myself.

The thought arises: Are we the cancer of planet Earth? These technological and economic needs look indiscriminate and hungry, greedy, randomly attempting to satisfy insatiable desires. I am still raw from being the host of a similarly unconscious entity, and it pains me to think I might be participating in a parallel phenomenon around me. Could cancer be a microcosmic reflection of our relentless ravaging of resources? If so, does this also reflect some macroscopic life in the greater Universe? Does the disorder of cancer have its core action in patterns woven through the DNA of the cosmic flow?

This does not exactly make me feel safe in the Universe, but it does displace ingrained thoughts of cancer. If cancer is a part of the whole sacred mechanism, then, as I originally perceived more than a year ago, it is a particle of the golden light of God. Cancer on all scales is here because it is a part of everything else we behold. There can be no blame assigned to cancer if I'm not willing to take responsibility for my own unconscious, destructive conduct. I'm not comfortable with such a possibility. I tell myself *go easy;* this feels close to the bone, dangerous.

∞

A human being lives in the body of God, just as God dwells in the body of a human being. As humans strive to understand life in the body, manipulating atoms and electrons and quarks, they find the same design of tiny particles held in spacious energy fields deeper and deeper in the cellular system that gives form to the seemingly solid body. As they strive to find life in the Universe, they find the same patterns in the night sky, stars and planets held in orbit, moving through a vast expanse, farther and farther into space. When humans look up into the blackness of a starry night, they are looking into their own bodies. The microcosm mirrors the macrocosm, guiding humans to realize their destinies.

It is true: Even cancer is a part of the mystical design, for nothing can exist outside the Universe, and humans reflect all actions in the universal flow, the misty veil of their skin the only suggestion of separation.

There is a pattern of movement throughout time, space, and material structures. By becoming aware of the responsibility to witness this grand design, there are unsavory realities, inexpressible joys, and an awesome, auspicious silence...

NINETEEN

I want nothing to do with my former self, my pre-cancer reality. I want to allow all the room I can for the new, unrealized me to emerge. And at the same time, I have only past images of myself to draw on for strength. Glimpses of my former self derail my healing. Sometimes the image gives me information about the courage still available inside me, and at other times it cracks open the well of grief, emptying the former me into the unknown future.

I attempt to go back to work more than once, then I back out. I do not have it in me yet to face any demands other than my own healing, and I feel the demise of my once-intact integrity. It is a confusing time for me. I put my home on the market — the only piece of my material past that has made it through the storm — as if shedding the one thing left would get the attention of the Universe, forcing it to give me the new blueprint of my life.

Then, after too much energy spent and hopes of escape (mind you, I had no destination or plan, just *out of my old life),* it doesn't sell. It is, after all, 2008, and I have not even been fully aware that we are in the worst recession since the Great Depression. I am uncomfortable in my own skin; at times I'm calm and able to rest, and at others the fear takes over and pushes on my raw nerves. My impatience mixes confusingly with trying to pace myself. I find that I must embrace the idea of staying in Taos...indefinitely. I must do my best to plant my feet into solid ground, start to ask for more help to face the fear-inducing trauma, detach from the urge to control everything, and lay my life down to the powers that caress me in the simple, quiet moments. I unpack more of my life, rehang clothes in closets, spread out into every room of the house, as I relent into silence and stillness, the only tangible attributes in my life left to me.

⤜⤛⤜⤛⤜

The only way to get through this life with all its conditions is
    to kick, groan, spin open, go backward, go forward, run
    away as fast as your legs will go, only to be inhabited
    by a wild animal that can't possibly perform your
    latest flight
Then gently shed the masquerade
Find your center...again...surrender to limitations
That can only be set free by a voice so clear and strong its
    vibrations echo back
Around the bend
Like a life fully lived leaves a brilliant residue on those
    left behind

⤜⤛⤜⤛⤜

Humans fear the unknown. They want to know, to understand.
As noble as the quest to be informed by their Soul is, much of the
Universe cannot be explained with the limited words with which
they are given to work. So in their striving, they push and pull and
throw up their hands in dismay to the gods. When they finally have
worn themselves out, only then are they ready to listen.

Nilama is no exception. Her pushing, at points, saved her
life. Pushing too hard will bring her to her knees again. There is a
constant balance that must be honored; it will take time for her to
know the push is over; the breath no longer needs to be restricted at
every turn. What will bring her healing is patience—doing her best
to apply her newfound wisdom, working through the confusion of
annihilated boundaries, and praying again. Learning to listen
again. To live her way into the answers.

TWENTY

Poetry has been streaming through me for a year or more, as I struggle to find a way to reconcile my life.

I hear words that answer my call. I am so grateful to this voice in me, this tender healer and friend who has never left my side. It calls me always to stillness, and I'm beginning to trust that if I stay still, the answers will come in time—not my time, but the time of The Sacred.

How do you suppose I am to reconcile this life?
The cost of your love is the surrender of everything material
Yet you placed me here in this physical body
This worldly madness of the sleeping Soul
I feel the intense fear that moves most people into power
        and control
You tell me they are all you
I sense the judgment and loss
You tell me it is all an illusion
I see the pain and suffering
Yet you tell me it is not the truth
You gave me a mind and told me to keep it focused on
        your love
And I would be free

I don't understand this freedom right now
So can you tell me how to reconcile your love?

Silence
Silence is all I hear
Silence is the vibration of my heart
Silence is the space of love
Silence is the reconciliation

꧁꧂

TWENTY-ONE

I am not dead, but I certainly don't feel alive. The doctors tell me, year after year, "One more year and your bowels will be healed." I lose faith in them. I remember that the human body undergoes one complete round of cellular replacement every seven years. I decide that seven years is my own personal timetable to become fully healed — a generous amount of time that eases the pressure I place on my body to become whole again. My bowels are the worst of it: up to twenty-five bowel movements a day really shatters my tenuous patience. I seek specialists and complain, I cry and give up, then summon compassion for my digestive system, treating it like a newborn baby.

My Ayurvedic doctor, Sunil Joshi, is here from India, and I'm able to see him. At first he's worried about my traveling to see him in so fragile a state, but he agrees to see me.

It's a joy to see him. Dr. Joshi is surprised at how well I'm doing, under the circumstances, and acknowledges the amazing strength of my constitutional makeup, assuring me that *all things heal.* After more than a decade in his care, I love this man and trust him with my life.

He tells me, "You've done the right thing to have taken chemo and radiation...they saved your life. Now, let's get you back in balance and health."

I bathe in this lack of judgment. He takes great pleasure in calling me the phoenix that has risen from the ashes, in tandem with the familiar head swaggle of his culture. I smile at his easy way with me. He assures me that together we'll get my digestive system stronger.

As he reads my pulse, he finds that my digestive fire may have been greatly compromised, and he intuits my fragile emotional state—but my creative, transformational nature will sustain me through this healing time. "You are a very fortunate person," he reports, "with a beautiful, well-informed soul." I'm grateful for his expertise, born from ancient wisdom and handed down through his lineage. His professional knowledge gives me hope for as normal a life as I have the courage to imagine. With full faith in his precise instructions, I am able to begin to embrace an unburdened future.

∞

Destroying. Creating. Sustaining. The Universe and everything in it are ruled by these three processes. The body is created from the five elements, sustained by the pure utterance of universal mind, and eventually destroyed to make room for the new. Each of these experiences is fueled by Divine force. Call it Shiva, God, Divine Goddess; its vital tenacity necessitates change and beckons humans into a relationship with the Sacred. If they are willing to surrender, they will be guaranteed an opening into the greater life they are capable of living. If Nilama can allow what is present in her to be released, she will become an authentic voice—a voice that does not hold back from any scene in the play but embraces it and embodies what is being offered up by the Divine.

TWENTY-TWO

I'm sitting in the broadcast room of a radio station in Taos. The cancer group I am a part of is having a fundraiser. Chatting with the announcer before going on the air, I ask her not to introduce me as a *cancer survivor*. "But if I don't use that term, then what do I say when I talk about you and the cancer?" she asks.

"Say I *had cancer*," I reply.

This has been an issue for me from the very beginning of the cancer journey. I've never been fond of labels of any sort, and *cancer survivor* is no exception.

I did survive cancer, and for a while that thought brought about a sense of relief and, yes, accomplishment. It was no small thing I had participated in and lived through, but the question would rise up: Why would I choose a label that would leave me only partially healed? Had I lived through cancer to always be "a survivor?" I want to reënter life a free Soul. For me, the label was too limiting, too closely associated with victimhood, and I'm having a hard enough time not being a victim without a label to nudge me along.

Not to mention how separate from the rest of the world the disease has already made me feel. I wonder why, with cancer, we get this lifelong identity of survivor. It smells slightly of manipulation, money, politics, and commercialism. And what about the people who have died of cancer? I believe the label negates their lives, their challenges, and their passing: They died. They did not survive. They failed. Not being heroes, they can't be a part of the group. Do we not separate enough from one another without having to create more distance with labels? Or is it death we disavow?

I also choose not to identify with the words "fight" and "war." There is already so much violence that identifying with more aggression weakens me and leaves me feeling like a bystander, rather than an enthusiastic soldier, caught in a deadly crossfire.

I feel like a tsunami hit me. How in the world could I, in this tiny body, "fight" a tsunami? I'd had to surrender and participate with the force that engulfed my life, and believe that there was some goodness housed in the storm. I still have to surrender. I know I'll get knocked around, and maybe I'll die, but to fight a foe that no one really understands or can control seems ineffective at best. It will take more than fighting to live. I will have to trust the process of my life, my intuition guided by a force far greater than myself, and trust the words "I choose to align my new self with my Soul."

⋅⋙◈⋘⋅

Have you ever watched a red-tailed hawk as it cruises the
     open sky?
It catches every whisper of air for its use
It is free, able and aware of

How to capture every note on the scale
Like symbols created solely for the expression of flight
When we speak from purity of light
And we are heard
All who listen are in flight with us
Like geese in formation heading south
In the one there is all

⋘⋙

The great challenge of the human race is to not separate from others or from the love of God that resides in each one's heart. It is tempting to create borders and use terms of triumph to distinguish one group from another, to build safety where none can be found; but in the end, the shared vulnerability of each body and Soul cannot be denied. Human beings are united through suffering, joy, and love. All experiences are equal to the Divine One, each having its own special influence on the innocent nature of humans.

Nilama is traversing fine lines, discerning with the intricate instrument of her own healing. How she embodies herself will be significant in the years of healing ahead. The idea of freedom rings through her being, and the desire to not be labeled makes the cure more possible and liberates her to heal completely.

When one being chooses consciously, it restores faith for others to choose for themselves the level of healing they wish to attain. This choice will be transported into the web of all lives, for all time. Healing the wounded Soul is the goal; this healing is in the magical art of dying before you die, in each person's authentic path that dissolves into the insoluble profundity of life and death.

TWENTY-THREE

I am at the office of my gynecologist, Shanti Mohling. She has a new resident working with her. We're in the familiar room where, over the past years, Shanti has tended to my vulnerable and delicate interior body. I am answering the new resident's questions as we go over the history of the cancer. At one point, I cannot answer her question in detail. When she asks me why, I tell her that my surgeon was not very forthcoming about giving me details he didn't think I needed to know, which was almost everything. She asks me his name and I tell her. There's a slight pause. Then she says, "You may want to know that a group of residents got together and refused to study under him anymore, because of his abusive treatment of patients. He's no longer at that hospital."

The first thing I feel is validation. Throughout my time in his care, he had made me feel that I was being overly sensitive and demanding, making a big deal out of nothing. After all, he was a great surgeon and I shouldn't question him or his judgments, even regarding my own body. The next thing that strikes me is the mysterious flow that must be in synergistic harmony to put all the intricate details in place, dancing in the dust of ages, to bring this information directly into my path. I'm reminded of all the divine interventions in my life and how each one has been a partner in my healing. Will knowing that he has been judged by his peers as unprofessional, and that action has been taken against him, bring me another layer of healing? Perhaps. The validation alone is healing, but knowing that someone has taken up the case against him, I feel a righteousness on behalf of his many unsuspecting patients. I am not naïve enough to suppose that he's not practicing elsewhere, but the fact that justice has shed light on him, well, that's a good thing.

I remember my first follow-up colonoscopy back in Wisconsin. The doctor who performed the procedure came in afterward to sit face-to-face, to go over the results of the colonoscopy, and answer any of my questions. There was a dramatic difference in patient protocol in this hospital from where I had been. There were no outstanding issues, which was a relief, and at the end of our conversation, he confirmed something that I could never have found out from anyone but somebody with an inside view of my body. The work that was done to remove my rectum was superb, he said, and he added that he had never seen its match.

It brings me closer now to resolution with the original surgeon; even if he was a difficult person, he had done excellent work.

I'm not sure the end justified the means, but now he's been uncovered. He paid whatever price he had to pay in his life, and although it will take more time, I will eventually put the matter to rest.

⟨ornament⟩

I must wholeheartedly choose to cut the cord of violent
    memories
Let the life bleed slowly out of them
And as they lie dried and shriveled beside me
Take them up into sacred hands and honor them
Give them into the earth and let them feed me in a new way
For they are me or
At least a part of me that I could not and will not clear
    from my
Heart's forgiving wings

⟨ornament⟩

*Nilama and the surgeon never trusted each other. They remained
suspicious and separated. Her holistic approach scared him; his
all-powerful stance disempowered her. They found no place to meet
without fear and power blocking them. Courting death, he had
entered the cavity of her body, wrapped his hands around her
slippery bowels and transported them to rest in a bowl of fluid
before extracting the organ that housed the cancer. Finally he
returned them to her body, his confidence finding a field to plow.
Even this intimate act could not diminish the distance between
them, because for him, it was this very act that kept him at bay.*

    *Nilama was in his territory, an immigrant in an unknown
land, speaking another language; he held the key that opened
doors, but the locks were rusty. He could not overcome his claim to
self-righteous authority. They departed as they began: strangers,
foreign to each other.*

There is a revolution at hand for strangers such as these to learn to communicate, listen and understand the cultures that thrive on both sides of the artificial wall—in this case, between holistic and allopathic medicine. There is a movement in the under-pinnings of life, a shift that could put fear and power aside and unite one side with the other, in service to those who matter more than frail egos, greed, and misunderstandings: the patients. The borders could be crossed by greater awareness, new alliances made in compassion, benefiting all who are involved. The Souls that are able to bring this to fruition are already in motion. The time is ripe, and as always, these events must be lived into, with conscious choices made and outcomes revealed.

TWENTY-FOUR

Why did you get cancer?"

"How did you get cancer?"

"Have you figured out the one thing that gave you cancer?"

These kinds of questions would leak out, whether consciously or unconsciously, from people's mouths. When asked with conscious compassion, they instilled in me curiosity enough to find an answer. When asked with a tone of blame or judgment, they created momentary shame.

It would take years for me to weave these questions into answers that fit my experience.

Rectal cancer. At first, it was difficult to allow the two words that defined my experience to pass through my lips. Putting the word cancer with rectum left most conversations silent and awkward as I watched people's minds connect the dots and then be stumped as to how to proceed, possessed by paralytic nerves in their own bodies.

That left the other uncomfortable conversation: "Why did you get cancer?" I knew these conversations were either bringing unity through compassion and awareness or they were creating a void I could not bridge. I began to be able to discern between the different inquiries and noticed that one was filled with fear. If I would answer why, or how, or try to name that one thing that brought cancer into my life — like that I was raised in Wisconsin, a state that has the highest rate of colorectal cancer in the United States; or that as a child I had run through fogs of DDT that was used to kill mosquitoes in the marsh near our neighborhood; or if I would recall this or that, trying to ease not only them but myself with an answer — I found myself feeling distanced, each of us unconsciously staking a claim for camps in which the other could not or would not live.

On one level, they were weighing in as to how close to cancer they might be in their life, using my answers to seek relief from their own fears of getting cancer. I felt empty after these conversations, until I realized all they were doing was trying to feel safe. I thought how real and frightening cancer is in our world and how absolutely reasonable it is to want to create a buffer between them and me and cancer's growing tentacles. I dug for compassion to accompany all of us in this conversation. I also realized that I neither could nor would carry this burden of fear for them, allowing myself to be marginalized for their sense of safety. So eventually, when asked about cancer in a particular tone, I confessed that I didn't know why I got cancer and that I couldn't make them feel safe by guessing the cause. An uncomfortable answer to a discomforting question.

The antithesis of the same inquiry was much more enticing to me. It's not easy to describe the difference, but when asked in a different tone, I found myself contemplating more deeply how I would honestly answer this question for myself. The first layer of revelation was that I thought I

had prayed to understand suffering, because that's exactly
what I had done. Through my many years as a massage
therapist, I had always been attracted to those in great pain
and suffering or facing death. I had worked in hospice, with
cancer and AIDS patients, people in car accidents, and even
those with multiple personalities, always with enhanced
insight as to how people brought themselves to the pain
they were in. I realized that this goal I had prayed for—to
understand suffering—had been reached. I now understood suffering from dwelling inside it, and I know that
it is the grace of God and Goddess combined that carries
us through such times of hardship. Continuing to linger
in my curiosity allowed time and space for another answer
to emerge.

The answer I live with today, in full embrace, is
that my experience with cancer, and all its attendant trials,
belongs to this life. It belongs to me. Like everything in my
life that has conspired to enlarge my Soul, cancer is housed
in the translucent diameter of me. And through that
answer, as through most simple solutions that unburden
me of complexity, deeper healing is made available. The
completion of the quest to understand why cancer entered
my life has great power now and inspires new levels of
awareness. I am alive to the reality that whatever comes my
way need not be judged, only accepted for what it is. This
includes me. I am not to blame. The sacred design of my
human life lifts me out of the muddy waters of my ego. I
am cleansed by this answer's profound elegance.

⋅∽◇◇◇◠⋅

I prayed to understand compassion
I prayed to understand the pain I witnessed in the world
I could not bring together the torn ragged edges of God's love
      and suffering
So I prayed for courage...
Until the gods took notice and sent the dark angel of cancer
      to answer my prayers
Beyond my measure of courage, this angel tugged
Compassion came and dissolved into indefinable pools
      of pain
That she stirred with her intentions to free my doubts of
      love's existence.
For all my wanting to let go
I could not fully release into her trust
So she cupped her hands ever so gently
Around my reluctant heart
And held it beating
My interior eyes flew wide and met her wild gaze
There I was: fiercely, unbearably free
I relinquished my hold on this life
Then I grasped it back
And in my regret, lay my body to the Earth and wept

⋅∽◇◇◇◠⋅

Sacred vibrations create primordial sound in the Universe. This
reverberation will coalesce to shape letters; letters form words;
words form sentences. This energetic gathering is brought forth by

the command of the Great Lord. Words are holy. Every word carries within it causal implications that vary depending on the tone. The tone reveals the intention of the one speaking; therefore, the exact same words can convey entirely different meanings. They can separate or they can unite; even the time and place the words are released has great impact on their being received and heard.

Human emotions tend to rule people's words, and every human Soul knows the impact of words. The intense compassion required to allow for the imperfections within the use of words, and all they convey, is paramount to the experience of awakening. It is not what goes into a mouth that nourishes humanity, but what comes out of it.

TWENTY-FIVE

Until I find a cancer group that uses different language about this disease and its impact on people's lives, I feel angry about the words used to define the experience of cancer. In particular, the answer to a common question really gets to me. I have asked it, and heard it asked, many times: "When will you lose the fear of cancer returning?"

The answer I've been given repeatedly is, "Never." It never goes away. That really pisses me off. Will I have to live with this fear the rest of my life? Will the fear of cancer disrupt the blood flow through the joy of a normal life — even now that, with five years of repeated checkups behind me, I have been given a clean bill of health? What a horrible prison I'll be confined to, along with every other person who has had cancer. No wonder it's compelling to form a separated safe group and label it. That way we don't have to feel alone in the agony of such a life sentence. Connecting to those who are already bound to us by such a constraining contract is comforting. But there must be another way. I have no idea how, but I'm not going to let cancer rule the rest of my life by allowing it to lurk inside every shadow.

The answer for me comes while in conversation with a friend who had lived through breast cancer. She'd been talking to a client who had cancer, and he had asked her the famous question. As we talk, I realize I'm not living in fear of cancer returning. The fear is gone. How did this happen? As I contemplate this, I realize it was when I faced the undeniable, intimate reality of my own death. Breathing in massive levels of pain and suffering, then being spared death's exhale, has given me an advantage in the death department. I know I will die of something—maybe cancer, maybe something else.

Most assuredly, I do not cherish the idea of Soul-piercing pain again, but I concede that I have no control over how I die. The energy I put toward discovering life is enhanced by the surrender of claiming that the moment of death is a glorious extension of what resides in my heart. For it is peace I embrace, at least from this seemingly secure place of witness. I know how easily I can lie to myself, so I can't say that fear won't get its claws into me in my final days. Like a Shinto warrior, I still practice the reality of having a good death—one into which I can release my life with as little regret as possible and as much love as I can muster for the transition. But with the knowledge of a trial run, I know there will be moments reviewed that will leave me wanting. So there must be honest compassion. Compassion is my key to freedom, and I pray I have many years to practice. I need it.

Nilama has been tempered. It is time to meet her Self and witness cancer's handiwork.

⤳⤳⟨❈⟩⤝⤝

I turned a corner on the street today and
Ran face-first into an old friend...
She appears to have traveled a long way to get here and
Yet here she is
The same but different
The journey through time gave way to smoother edges and
Subtler tones
She has been someplace you don't take others with you
But you know some have gone before you
It is written in ancient tongues and
Shaped in metaphors
Like the razor's edge and the fire of transformation...
It is shadowy in her, I see
She knows but she doesn't know
She is still afraid to say
But no matter
I love her as I have always loved her
And it is my great good fortune
To call her my own

⤳⤳⟨❈⟩⤝⤝

TWENTY-SIX

I am sitting with Shanti, my gynecologist, in her office. I cry as she tells me she will be leaving Taos. Crying is not a new thing between us. Over the years I cried at each visit, my emotional walls torn down by her direct and honest eyes. I do not want her to go. She was my doctor before cancer and has been with me for the past seven years through the ordeal; she's one of the few doctors I've completely trusted. She has always listened with focused attention and respect for my holistic views, and together we've sought solutions to my multitude of delicate problems. She once said to me with a big smile and a wink, as she performed a rectal exam, that as sisters, we must look after each other.

Today is no different, as she supports me one more time in her office to follow my instincts with this book. "Most women I know who have had breast cancer and refused chemo are dead. There is not enough written about the obstacle that the fear of drugs creates for those who easily could have lived by using them, and continued their healing through holistic medicine. You have a great story to tell about the path you chose and you are living proof that these options are viable and real."

I promise her I will do my best.

Soon there will be very little that remains of cancer's demands on me, and the conversations that once consumed my every thought will dissipate. I have dreamed of this time of freedom from cancer's control over my life, but the prospect of losing Shanti's friendship, beauty, and wisdom tears a tiny wound of sadness in my heart; I sew it up tenderly with golden threads of gratitude.

I have noticed subtle changes in my gratitude. Where once (eons ago, it seems) I would wake with exuberant energy for all life could bring, grateful that life seemed to coöperate with my every desire. I now have a more refined experience of this auspicious attribute.

Now the bliss of life going my way is stirred into the direct understanding that things were never going my way in the first place. I never had control over the events of my life, only how I embraced them. Every detail of my life is complete in and of itself: the pain and suffering, grief and loss, are held in the same arms as joy and receiving, love and connection. This reality lends me to the world in a new way. Less frivolous, more grounded. Less confined, but needing less space in the world. Less separated by fear from all that lives in this majestic Universe. I may not appear as bouncy and gay as I once was, but inside...inside I am privy to the darkness that dwells in the light, and I can behold a landscape complete with the awareness of all that the fierce Goddess offers, and my sense of gratitude is immersed in her blessings.

∞

Each Soul makes pacts with the possibilities in life. These alliances will bring every Soul into the play they came to produce. Nilama went the way of Western medicine, simultaneously applying the healing arts known to her and the healers in her life. The many years of fostering good health helped carry her through.

Once the Western model was complete, Nilama was free to delve deeply into more spiritually based and personally designed healing systems. These systems offer her healing on all levels. Other Souls will make their own appropriate alliances for their healing. Some will refuse Western medicine and some will die without it. Others will report miraculous healing through other, less invasive treatments. The important issue is that each path has profound impacts on the Soul's journey and creates wholeness in the Soul of God.

Every choice is magnificent, each one a true expression of that Soul's authentic voice. Humans learn from each other's choices —this is how the fear is corralled, because as people share their miraculous journey, from a forgiving and compassionate place, the fear consumes less space. People can witness the outcomes of others' choices and find courage—the courage to live or the courage to die.

TWENTY-SEVEN

Many of my concepts about life have been turned upside down, rearranged or left by the wayside. One in particular fascinates me: I used to notice that when people were telling me how fortunate they were that everything in life had gone their way, and that they had never been sick or suffered (and how blessed they were in being spared such tragedies), it made me wonder at the purpose of all the suffering in the world — particularly, of course, my own. What value did cancer have in my life? What would be the purpose of seeking such answers, if there even were answers? I would feel sad for myself and then I would feel sad for them, because deep within me there is an incredible freedom that living through the challenges of great suffering has given me.

I look back now on how I thought I'd never have to go through any health issues because I took such good care of myself. Certainly, illness happened to people who didn't live as cleanly as I did. I had a false sense of power, of my own invincible self — one that protected me from my true vulnerability here on Earth, in this fragile body. I trusted completely that whatever I asked my body to do, it would do, and I that I could bend my body to my will.

Now, I am humbly bent to my body's will, and I must say it is a kinder master than the fierce will of my mind. And slowly, slowly, my mind gives way to its new teacher. I do not believe that I am invincible, or that nothing will ever happen to me again. Substantial wisdom extends from listening to my body's inner rhythms, like a gentle monk tending to the demanding tyrant in me who lives in constant fear of not being enough — of not deserving my own love — and who believes that amassing enough thickness will make me feel safe.

Pain has split a thin crack in my being, and within it lies the yearning of the Mother to bring me home. She feeds the longing of my Soul to embrace the pain that creates an expedient access to the Divine. The light of Her grace is blinding, but when I stay present in Her magnetic luminosity, my awareness widens and deepens, and a view that renders me available to all possibilities is present before me. I have sought this view all my life. I have wondered and longed for and prayed to see beyond what my human eyes believe to be solid and real, to peer into the finer, more translucent vision that my heart and Soul can reveal. The pain of this imagined separation is surely as bad as the burns on my body from radiation; and paradoxically, it is the suffering of my body that answered my call. Cancer, suffering, has brought me closer to the divinity that dwells within me, and the love that fills this simple being who I Am.

Honestly, this is why I kept going to cancer groups, to find others who may have similar thoughts about this connection created through cancer. I wanted to have conscious discussions that could help me shift the old paradigm of fear into one of healing and greater vision. I needed, and still do need, others to guide me away from my smallness. I believe that is why we are not islands unto ourselves. We need others to help us remember our greatness and to embrace our authentic, beautiful gifts. One way or another, we are designed to connect.

∞

Nilama no longer sees herself as a victim but as someone given the opportunity for deeper understanding through suffering, and now she can heal old wounds and connect to others with a refined thread of gold. The connection she has longed for is growing, for herself and for society, because with the tolerance learned through suffering, she and many others can move about in the world with greater ease and less fear.

The gift of acceptance changes anger to forgiveness and violent fears to quiet compassion. This is freedom in its highest form.

TWENTY-EIGHT

I lay in my early-morning bath, performing the daily Ayurvedic ritual of massaging oil into my skin to aid my nervous system and bring balance to my doshas. The oil seeps through open pores, soothing me from the night's physical memories. Writing this book has stirred old thoughts and residues of trauma. Medical PTSD, the disability court calls it.

I recall the first time I was able to face the trauma. I was in Wisconsin, still living with my parents, and I was working with a therapist. Tammy and I were cut from the same cloth, and I felt a deep, immediate kinship with her. The day she mentioned trauma I remember thinking, what is she talking about? Trauma? I don't have any trauma. I'm fine. I just need to get back to living.

I returned weekly to her office. One day she read me a children's story about a little being with a pie-shaped slice cut from its round, ball-like body, who goes on adventures to find its missing piece. I wondered, do I have a missing piece? I looked down, and my hand caressed the pillow at my elbow. Tiny mirrors held by colorful embroidered threads were sewn into the plush Indian fabric. It struck me as quite beautiful. That act brought me to the present moment, and I was awake. Awake to the beauty and pain and wisdom that reside within me. Heavy waves of tears flowed for what had been cut from my body and my life.

I surrendered to the grief. I wrote down everything I had lost through the cancer. It filled every line — no borders, no space, back and front — of eight pages of paper. I felt devastated by the list. I remembered something I had once read: Suffering is measured by the amount of loss.

Before I was able to recognize trauma's ability to annihilate reality and blast boundaries to smithereens, I would test family and friendships, entangle myself in relationships I had no business being in, and create scenarios of drama. Each time, the present reality I would strive to govern tangled with the reptilian brain, caught in past moments of torment.

The medical trauma my body was responding to was the result of an overload of events that the nervous system had not registered or released. It held me in the past. Its goal was to protect me from further injury until I could manage to resolve the built-up trauma, but it also prevented me from touching my life in the here and now. It hid underground and usurped my reality. Once I discovered it, I found trained therapists to guide me out of its shadowy reactions. Biofeedback with Nancy Hazen was especially helpful. The healing process required me to stay diligent to the present: Outdoor walking, yogic breathing exercises, and the pure intention to pay attention taught me to recognize trauma's approach and redirect myself to present time.

Now, the painful memories of my unconscious acts while in trauma have diminished in strength, and the shame they once evoked in me creates only a dusty beam of light that requires no attention. It has taken over seven years to gain a perspective wide enough to write, for compassion and healing to define the experience, and like the moment with the intricate beauty of the pillow, to awaken me to the present moment.

I have traveled a great distance on this path with cancer. I am not the same shape, my metal beaten thin, tempered by fire. All I wish for now is simple peace, forgiveness, and the courage to stand in this life that was created for me to live, in service to the love that creates us all.

⋯⋙⊗⊗⋘⋯

A sage offered me this option:
Thank all those who have caused you pain because it
    brought you closer to me...
It must be said or I remain a slave to the tyrant of my fears,
    chained at a breath's distance from my Birthright
So, I will risk the unreal safety of fear's confinement, for one
    moment of spacious peace
Thank you cancer
I accept the mystical purpose of your impact on this life
Thank you cancer
I accept that my soul invited you to my table
Thank you cancer
I accept this stark vulnerability
Thank you for bringing me closer to the fullness of me
And although I do not know where I am going or what to do...
Or how this story can end in a pleasant way
Is it not now glorious and free?

⋯⋙⊗⊗⋘⋯

EPILOGUE

"It was hours post-op and I hadn't fully reëmerged into consciousness. I was in pain and terrified. As I opened my eyes, there stood my friend Christine, like an apparition. Tears started pouring from my eyes. She simply climbed into my fancy hospital bed, tubes and wires and all, and held me. I knew she knew. She was the only one who knew."

— Chaitanyo

The last week that I was writing this manuscript, I took Chaitanyo to the hospital to have a bowel resection, due to cancer. The day after his surgery, I walked into his room, and in his groggy state and torment, he said, "This is just nuts." I understood viscerally what he meant.

The nurse, advising him to get up (which he flatly refused to do), left the room. My intuition guided my actions. I slid beside him in the bed and placed my right hand on his belly to do Reiki, as he rested his head in the hollow of my shoulder, against my breast. Tears released as his whole body melted into mine, and the terror and pain gave way to rest.

I left the hospital deeply moved by the trust my friend had honored me with that day. My hopes of being available to help heal cancer patients with compassion and self-born knowledge was now a reality.

It was a powerful day for both of us.

MY SWEET CRUSHED ANGEL

You have
not danced so badly, my dear,
trying to hold hands with the Beautiful One

You have waltzed with great style, my sweet, crushed angel,
to have ever neared God's heart at all

Our partner is notoriously difficult to follow, and even His
best musicians are not always easy to hear

So what if the music has stopped for a while
So what if the price of admission to the Divine is out of reach tonight

So what, my sweetheart, if you lack the ante to gamble for real love.

The mind and the body are famous for holding the heart ransom,
but Hafiz knows the Beloved's eternal habits. Have patience
for He will not be able to resist your longings
and charms for long.

You have not danced so badly, my dear,
trying to kiss the Magnificent
One

You have actually waltzed with tremendous style
my sweet, O my sweet
crushed
angel.

Poem by Hafiz
Translated by Daniel Ladinsky
Love Poems from God, Penguin Compass Press

The complete poems that inspired this book
can be found in Christine Sherwood's first book of poetry:
HELP ME REMEMBER WHO I AM

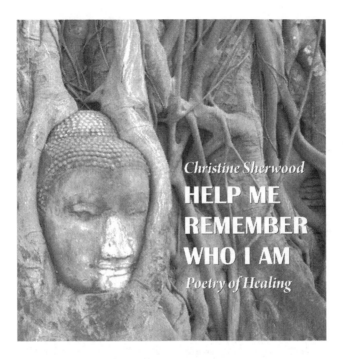

Christine Sherwood
HELP ME
REMEMBER
WHO I AM
Poetry of Healing

"These poems tell the story of a soul desired by God,
washed and honed, perfected to service in the world of
suffering and separation, that rises like the phoenix
from the flames of transformation."
– Susan P. Blevins

Please visit: www.christine-sherwood.com

ABOUT THE AUTHOR

Christine Sherwood, born in Wisconsin in 1957, originally moved to the mountains of Northern New Mexico in 1977. In 1989, she moved to a small desert community in Nevada to raise her daughter, Tracy, hiking and wandering the Red Rock Canyon lands.

In 1991, Christine graduated from massage school and in 1995 returned to New Mexico to begin her teaching career in the healing arts.

She created her own CEU class for massage therapists, "Bones of the Earth," which she taught nationwide from 1998 until 2006.

She presently lives in Northern New Mexico. The spacious peace of the high-desert sky, the beauty of the mountains, the sun, and the trees feed her body and soul.

Christine is available for speaking engagements.

Made in the USA
Charleston, SC
23 October 2016